Langford Lovell Price

Industrial peace, its advantages, methods and difficulties

A report of an inquiry made for the Toynbee Trustees

Langford Lovell Price

Industrial peace, its advantages, methods and difficulties
A report of an inquiry made for the Toynbee Trustees

ISBN/EAN: 9783337221928

Printed in Europe, USA, Canada, Australia, Japan

Cover: Foto ©Suzi / pixelio.de

More available books at **www.hansebooks.com**

INDUSTRIAL PEACE

ITS

ADVANTAGES, METHODS, AND DIFFICULTIES

A REPORT

OF AN INQUIRY MADE FOR THE TOYNBEE TRUSTEES

BY

L. L. F. R. PRICE

FORMERLY SCHOLAR OF TRINITY COLLEGE, OXFORD

With a Preface

BY

ALFRED MARSHALL

PROFESSOR OF POLITICAL ECONOMY IN THE UNIVERSITY OF CAMBRIDGE

London

MACMILLAN AND CO.

AND NEW YORK

1887

THIS report is reprinted (with additions) from a paper entitled "Sliding "Scales and other Methods of Wage-Arrangement in the North of England," which was read before the Statistical Society of London on 21st December, 1886, and inserted in the *Journal* of the Society for March, 1887. The author, therefore, desires to express his thanks to the Society for granting its permission to the publication of the report in its present form.

" We should do all that in us lies to establish Boards of Conciliation in
" every trade when the circumstances—economic or moral— are not entirely
" unfavourable. . . . . . But, notwithstanding failures and obstacles, I
" believe these Boards will last : and more than that, I believe that they have in
" them the possibilities of a great future."

ARNOLD TOYNBEE—*Lecture on " Industry and*
" Democracy," delivered in 1881 *to audiences*
of working-men at Newcastle, &c. Cf. " The
" Industrial Revolution," p. 201.

PREFACE.

THE following Report by Mr. Price is the first publication issued by the Toynbee Trustees. The reasons which led to the establishment of that Trust are described better than I could do it myself in the following extracts from a letter by Mr. Alfred Milner, one of those who knew Arnold Toynbee best, and in whose life he is still living:—

"Among his old friends no circumstance added a more "poignant sorrow to the great grief of his loss than the "feeling that, except as far as the ineffaceable impression "on a few minds went, he had left nothing behind him that "would perpetuate his influence, or even give those who "had not known him the faintest conception of the great "character so early lost to the world. Under these circum-"stances the desire to create some sort of memorial was "even stronger than it is in the ordinary case of the death "of a great man, who leaves some visible record of his own "behind him in the shape of accomplished work. All sorts "of things were proposed—a studentship of Political "Economy at Oxford, a prize, a workman's hall, or some "such institution as has actually grown up, with his name "attached to it, at the East End. What finally decided us "to choose the present form of the Trust was the desire to "connect the memorial both with the study of Political "Economy in its social aspects, to which he devoted the "scholar-half of himself, and with his work among the "artisan population of our great cities to which he gave the "other, the missionary-half. These two characters, so "inextricably blended in his disposition, his scheme of life, "and his actual performance, and at the same time so

a 2

" characteristic of what is best in the social movement of
" our time among the educated classes, we hoped to com-
" memorate by a series of lectures, to be delivered not at
" one place, but alternately at different great industrial
" centres, wherever there might seem to be a real demand
" for them—lectures dealing with political economy on its
" social side, at once instructive and inspiring. They were
" to be, if I might use the phrase, *pioneer* lectures, breaking
" open the road in different places, along which others, if
" there was interest shown and zeal to turn that interest to
" good account, might subsequently march. The lecturers
" were to be the forerunners of the university extension
" movement in political economy, teaching it, always, in
" Toynbee's spirit; and in sending them out we hoped to
" benefit both the industrial centres, which they were to visit
" and to enrich with the learning of the university, and the
" university itself, to which they would return strengthened
" by that experience and touch with actual life, the flesh and
" blood of economics, which could be gained nowhere else so
" well as in the industrial centres. The lecturer was thus to
" be both a teacher and a learner, bringing back fresh
" knowledge of a new kind to the seat of learning, in
" exchange for that which he had taken with him, or rather
" bringing back his old knowledge mellowed by experience.
" Hence the provision, which is an essential part of our
" scheme, that the lecturer shall not be overwhelmed with
" teaching and class-work, but shall be so amply supplied
" with means and with leisure as to be able to make a fresh
" contribution to economic science in the shape of a special
" study of some point illustrated by the industrial life of the
" particular community in which he teaches."

I knew Arnold Toynbee first when he had just begun to
lecture at Oxford on Economics. He was full of enthusiasm
for his work, but also he was a little anxious about it; as all
earnest people are when the responsibility first presses on
them of giving opinions that may influence the actions of
others on a subject which is so subtle and intricate, and yet

for which academic training by itself is so inadequate a preparation. He had indeed been brought at an early age into contact with the realities of life, and had been impelled in the first instance to economic studies by seeing with his own eyes, and hearing with his own ears, the results of that physical and moral degradation and suffering which are caused by poverty. He was struck by the fact that the sources of evil have their roots very far below the surface, and that what at first sight appears to be the best remedy for them, scarcely ever turns out to be the best, and in fact often aggravates them.

But he was impatient with the attitude of passionless observation, which he thought many of the older economists took. Some of their studies of the way in which competition works itself out, seemed to him like the exercises of a chess player, delighting in brilliant combinations, and without a sigh for the knights or the pawns who may be sacrificed on the way. Economic problems were to him pregnant with the fates of the suffering toilers whom he knew so well, and he could not bear to have them treated as mere exercises of analytical reasoning.

But as time went on he somewhat changed his attitude towards the earlier economists. He learned to understand their difficulties better, to see what led them at times to make assumptions which at first sight appear perversely unreal; and he got to distinguish their own opinions from those which are attributed to them by people who want to quote economic authority for partisan purposes. Gradually he settled himself down to work very much on the old fashioned lines, but giving prominence to historical studies, and never for a moment losing sight of the question whether it may not be possible to prevent any class from being so poor as to be debarred from a healthy, happy, and cultured life.

He had many sides, as the readers of the memoir of him by the Master of Balliol will know. But on the few occasions which I met him, the talk ran chiefly on social and economic questions. He was always brilliant in thought, eager in speculation; but his intellect, fresh and vigorous as it was, was not the chief part of him: the leading controlling strain of his character was emotional. He was thus the ideal modern representative of the mediaeval saint: strong every way, but with all other parts of his nature merged and contained in an earnest and tender love towards God and man.

I knew this in a way when talking to him; but I did not realise it fully till he had left us; not until I had been invited to Oxford to lecture in his place, and had got to see there how his life had influenced many of the best of those around him. As time goes on this influence spreads: in London and Cambridge no less than in Oxford his name is familiar as the watchword of a great movement. The mediaeval saint of whom he was the modern representative was St. Francis, the founder of a new order, the leader of a new and more direct attack on the evils of the age. In this modern age, as in earlier times, it is through his personal influence that the leader has made himself felt; and the new impulse that Toynbee gave was towards a more intimate personal contact of those who are well nurtured, well cultured and strong, with those who are ill nourished and ignorant and weak.

Such he was, and such his portrait would tell him to be if it could speak clearly. The frontispiece of the present volume is reproduced from the best likeness of him that there is; but it is not quite satisfactory, it does not adequately represent the beauty and strength of his character. It will however help those who knew him to freshen their own memories of him, and it will enable others to form some imperfect notion of what he was.

In complying with the request of the Trustees of the Toynbee fund to write a preface to Mr. Price's admirable Report, my chief thought has been how it would have given joy to Toynbee. It is work after his own heart on subjects in which he was deeply interested. He held that the organised warfare of strikes and lock-outs on a modern pattern was in some respects less evil than the old fashioned guerilla warfare, which attracted less public attention ; but which was really more bitter, and had more mean and cruel incidents in it. He welcomed the growing power of trades unions, because they brought generally the best men to the front, and clothed them with a grave responsibility, which was itself an education and fitted them to educate others by their leadership; and he welcomed the effect of public criticism which was brought to bear on both the belligerents when the war was carried on openly in the full light of the day. But he yearned for a time of Industrial Peace; and his praise of trades unions was never warmer than when he was speaking of the way in which they had promoted the growth of arbitration and conciliation. The chief purpose of this essay is to inquire how, without recourse to industrial war, wages may be adjusted to the varying circumstances of trade in such a way as will be held by both sides to be relatively fair.

An absolutely fair rate of wages belongs to Utopia. There is much to be learnt from trying with the Socialists to ascertain how far it is thinkable, and how far it is attainable. But these are not the questions which we are asked to consider by Mr. Price. It is sufficient to say that all socialistic schemes which have any claims to be practical avowedly involve a compromise; they do not venture to dispense entirely with material reward as an incentive to industrial energy, though they rely less on it and more on the sense of duty than our present system does. But this compromise prevents them from claiming to be logically thought out schemes of absolute fairness. Fairness then cannot be absolute, but must be a matter of degree. Even for the purpose of day-dreams we must deliberately frame our notions of equity in the distribution of wealth, with reference to the methods of industry, the habits of life, and the character of the people for whom we are trying to discover a realisable ideal. And much more must we do

this when we are trying to construct a working plan, which
will so accommodate itself to the actual conditions of
business as to be accepted in preference to the excitement of
conflict by people as they are, with all their hot impulses,
their combative instincts, and their inherited selfishness.

There may indeed be a question whether there is room
within these narrow limits for any useful definition of " a
" fair rate of wages." But the phrase is constantly used in
the market place; it is frequent in the mouths both of
employers and of employed; and almost every phrase in
common use has a real meaning, though it may be difficult
to get at. Those who use the phrase, when pressed to
explain it, often give an account that will not bear examination; but after the matter has been discussed for a time, the
meaning that is latent in their minds works itself to the
surface. This process seems to be going on with regard to
the phrase " a fair rate of wages." in spite of the hasty
contempt that has been poured on it by some economists;
and Mr. Price's essay will help the process forward.

The basis of the popular notion that there should be
given " a fair day's wage for a fair day's work,"[1] is that
every workman who is up to the usual standard of efficiency
of his trade in his own neighbourhood, and exerts himself
honestly, ought to be paid for his work at the usual rate for
that trade and neighbourhood; so that he may be able to
live in that way to which he and his neighbours in his rank
of life have been accustomed. But further, the popular
notion of fairness demands that he should be paid this rate
ungrudgingly, that his time should not be taken up in fighting
for it, that he should not be worried by constant attempts to
screw his pay down by indirect means. This doctrine is
modified by the admission that changes of circumstances
may require changes of wages in one direction or the other:
and again, the rule might not be held to apply to cases such

[1] See an instructive lecture with this title by Mr. Leonard Courtney,
given at Plymouth in 1879, and published in the twenty-fifth volume of
the " Fortnightly Review."

as that of needlewomen, where the customary wages are
too low to support a healthy life. But substantially it is
accepted and acted on in ordinary life: and it is so far
justified by economic analysis that it may be accepted as the
starting point of our present inquiry. Let us look at it a
little more closely.

If a carpenter has made a box, or a surveyor has made
a map of some land for us, we consider that he acts fairly
by us if he does not attempt to take advantage of our not
having made a bargain beforehand, or of our ignorance, or of
any special hold he may have over us; but charges us the
price of his services at the rate at which he would expect to
be able to dispose of them regularly to those who understand
his trade. In this we are not trying to settle according to
any absolute standard of justness how much of a carpenter's
labour ought to be paid as highly as an hour's work of the
surveyor. We are not inquiring whether the social system
which permits great inequalities in their usual rates of remuneration is the best possible : but taking the present social
system as it is, we want to know whether those with whom
we are dealing are doing their part to make it work smoothly.

The average rate of earnings of a surveyor is limited on
the one hand by the demand for a surveyor's work : but it is
determined chiefly by the difficulty and expense of acquiring
the knowledge and skill required for his work. The rate of
earnings which are required to induce a sufficient number
of people to become surveyors is, in economic phrase, the
" normal" rate of surveyors' earnings. This normal rate
has no claim to be an absolutely just rate; it is relative
to the existing state of things here and now. It might
be altered without any fundamental change in the rights
of private property; the normal earnings of a carpenter
and a surveyor might be brought much nearer together
than they are, by even so slight and easy an improvement
on our present social arrangements as the extending to
all persons of adequate natural ability the opportunity of
receiving the training required for the higher ranks of

industry. But we have to take things as they are; and as things are, the price at which a man in any trade can expect to get steady employment, from those who are good judges of the value of his work, is a tolerably well known normal rate. The surveyor or the carpenter who always charges about this rate to any customers, however ignorant, and without putting them to the trouble of beating him down, is said to do his business fairly.

Similarly a fair employer when arranging for the pay of a carpenter, does not try to beat him down, or take any indirect advantage of him; but, at all events under ordinary circumstances, offers at once whatever he knows to be the " normal" rate of pay for that man's work : that is the pay which he would expect to have to give in the long run for an equal amount of equally good work if that man refused to work for him. On the other hand he acts unfairly if he endeavours to make his profits not so much by able and energetic management of his business, as by paying for labour at a lower rate than his competitors; if he takes advantage of the necessities of individual workmen, and perhaps of their ignorance of what is going on elsewhere ; if he screws a little here and a little there; and perhaps in the course of doing this, makes it more difficult for other employers in the same trade to go on paying straight-forwardly the full rates. It is this unfairness of bad masters which makes trades unions necessary and gives them their chief force : were there no bad masters, many of the ablest members of trades unions would be glad, not indeed entirely to forego their organisation, but to dispense with those parts of it which are most combative in spirit. As it is, though at great expense to themselves and others, they succeed tolerably well on the whole in preventing individual masters from taking unfair advantages of individual men.

The starting point then in our search for the fair rate of payment for any task, in the limited sense of the word " fair" with which alone we are here concerned, may be found in the average rate that has been paid for it during

living memory ; or during a shorter period, if the trade has
changed its form within recent years. But this average rate
is often very difficult to determine ; and therefore for practical purposes it is generally best to take in lieu of it the rate
actually paid in some year when according to general
agreement the trade was in a normal condition.[2] This gives
very nearly the same result, and is more definite and less
open to dispute. It is then assumed as a starting point that
the rate at that time was a fair rate, or in economic phrase
that it was the normal rate ; that is, that it was about on a
level with the average payment for tasks in other trades
which are of equal difficulty and disagreeableness, which
require equally rare natural abilities and an equally expensive
training. And accepting this year as a normal year for the
trade implies an admission that the current rate of profits in
the trade was also normal. Differences in ability or in good
fortune may have been causing some employers to make very
high profits while others were losing their capital ; but taking
one with another it is supposed that at this standard time
their net receipts gave them interest on their capital, and
earnings for their own work in managing the business, at
the same rate as work in other trades which was equally
difficult and disagreeable, and which required equally rare
natural abilities and an equally expensive training.

But changes in the course of trade may require a considerable departure from this starting point. These changes
are of many different kinds. Some are gradual in action,
and work slowly for a long time in one direction. For
instance a new trade has at first normal wages higher than
other trades of equal intrinsic difficulty ; it is difficult
because it is unfamiliar. Gradually it becomes familiar, a
great many people have been brought up to it, and its wages
slowly sink to a lower level. Or, again, improvements in
machinery, which cause it to work more smoothly and with
less care, may lower the strain required for performing the
same nominal task, and thus lower the nominal rate of wage,

[2] See pp. 61, 69, 73, and 96 of Mr. Price's essay.

even though the payment for work involving a given strain, is stationary or rising. Or again, the mean level of the general purchasing power of money may be moving slowly upwards or downwards, in consequence of changes in the supply of the precious metals, or of gradual changes in the volume and character of banking and general business. All these are slow changes; there may be disputes as to the facts of the case : but when once they are clearly ascertained, the course is generally clear. Setting aside all questions as to the right of some to be rich while others are poor, it is " fair " that full effect should be given to these changes. For they have on their side natural forces so powerful that opposition to them cannot be successful for long : and it cannot as a rule be maintained even for a short time without recourse to the harsher measures of trade combinations— measures that involve war open or concealed between employers and employed, or between both and the purchasers of their wares. Industrial wars like other wars involve so much waste, that the net gain which they bring to the winners, if any, is much less than the net loss to the losers. And therefore the side which adopts measures of warfare in opposition to changes that are irresistible, is generally acting not only unwisely, but also unfairly.

It is, however, often difficult to know how far any set of tendencies is irresistible ; how far the causes now acting in one direction are likely to be overborne before long by others acting in the opposite. The presumption that it is part of the employer's business to undertake the risks of the trade, makes it very difficult to know how soon and how far he ought in fairness to concede to his men the full advantage of any improvement in the condition of trade, which may after all last but a short time ; and how soon and how far he may require of them a fall in wages to meet a drooping condition of trade which may be but temporary.

In the ordinary course of things the first benefit of an improvement in the demand for their wares goes to the employers ; but they are likely to want to increase their output while prices are high, and make high profits while they can. So they soon begin to bid against one another for extra labour; and this tends to raise wages and hand over some of the benefit to the employed. This transfer may be retarded, though seldom entirely stopped, by a combination among employers, or it may be hastened on by the combined action of the employed. As a general rule employers will be bound in fairness to yield at once in such a case a considerable part of their new profits in higher wages, without waiting till their men force it from them by warlike measures, which necessarily involve waste. Even if they succeed temporarily they will set going a spirit of contentiousness, and check the inflow of additional supplies of labour into their trade; the net gain which they get from refusing to yield will probably be small, while the net loss to the employed will be great; their action will be unfair. Fairness requires a similar moderation on the part of the employed. If they try to force wages so high as to leave a very scanty profit for their employers just at the time when they might expect to make their best harvest, capital will be discouraged from entering the trade; probably even many of those in it will leave it when work gets slack, even if they do not fail when the first touch of depression comes. The men will then find it difficult to get employment, and will probably thus lose more than all they have gained by their extreme demands, even if they should be successful in the first instance; the net gain to themselves will be little if any, the net loss to their employers will be very great; their claims will be unfair.

When trade declines, the loss in the first instance falls on employers; as prices generally rise before wages rise, so they fall before wages fall. The duties of the two sides are now reversed. The men ought in fairness to yield something without compelling their employers to fight for it; and nothing short of absolute necessity will make it fair for the employers to demand a reduction of wages so great as to cause much suffering to the employed, and drive many of

them out of the trade.   For such extreme demands will
bring them, even if temporarily successful, a very small net
gain in proportion to the net injury done to the employed.

Sometimes indeed, for tactical reasons, either side will
demand at first more than it expects to get; but though this
may be inevitable in a state of suppressed industrial warfare,
it is injurious to the common interests; it is fair only in the
sense in which everything is fair in war; it is unfair from the
point of view of industrial peace.

From that point of view again it is unfair for the men to
spring claims for an advance on an employer suddenly, when
he has just taken important term contracts under heavy
penalties; it is unfair for the employer to take advantage of
the fact that the men have had irregular employment and are
short of money, and to use this as a lever for compelling
them to work at a lower rate than the necessities of the case
demand.

These are typical instances of what is unfair; there are
many other classes of action which are ungenerous, and
others again which would be avoided by an employer who
acted up to the highest standard of unselfishness.   But with
these we are not directly concerned just at present.   We
have before us now only the narrow and limited inquiry, how
far it is possible for frank dealing in a friendly spirit between
employers and employed to remove those unfair dealings,
and suspicions of unfair dealings, which are the chief causes
of industrial war.   The facts and the arguments which are
brought before us in the following pages give reasons for
thinking that it may go very far.

The best method is that of Conciliation.[3]   This will
always be associated with the name of Mr. Mundella, who
has done more than anyone else to develop its strength and
overcome its difficulties.   In the ideal form of this plan,
delegates of employers and employed meet from time to
time with the intention of speaking with perfect openness,
avoiding everything like special pleading; each side trying to

[3] See pp. 71 and 72, also pp. 37, &c.

put itself into the point of view of the other side, and
resolving to demand nothing that does not appear reasonable when looked at from that other side.

They have two kinds of inquiry before them. In the one
they move, so to speak, horizontally : they bring under comparison different kinds of work at the same time. Thus in
mining, different rates have to be made for different kinds of
coal, and even for different seams of the same coal.[4] While
in some trades, as for instance, the hosiery trade, prices for
many thousand different kinds of work have to be agreed
on. And, the most intricate matter of all, allowance has
sometimes to be made for differences in the condition of the
plant of different manufacturers; a rate which is fair in a
factory which has all the latest improvements, is bound to be
unfair in a badly organised factory with antiquated machinery. But, complex as these details are, this horizontal
levelling of prices is comparatively easy; an agreement is
often obtained with surprising quickness where there is a
frank and genial disposition on both sides. The difficulty is
much greater when the exigencies of the time require the
price of the standard task—whether paid by the day or by
the piece—to move above or below its standard level, and
the calculations have to be made vertically instead of
horizontally.

It is clear that since working men get much less good
from a temporary rise of their wages above their usual level,
than they do harm from an equal fall below it, therefore the
fluctuations of wages should be less in proportion than those
of the profits of the employers as a body. But here it may
be right to make some difference between specialised and
non-specialised workmen : skilled miners cannot turn to
other work when mining is depressed without great loss, and
their numbers cannot be quickly increased when there is a
great demand for their work : their fortunes are more
intimately bound up with mining than those of the labourers
and others who work on the surface of the mines. It is

[4] See pp. 38 and 76.

therefore in accordance with sound principle that the wages
of underground men should follow the fluctuations of the
trade more closely than those of "surface men."[5] Next it is
not fair that the workmen should share in the good or ill
fortunes of the particular firm by which they are employed,
unless they have made a special agreement to do so. Profit
sharing arrangements when well managed are a gain to all
concerned : but it is difficult to make them, and more difficult
to keep them up. They require a good deal of mutual
knowledge and confidence on the part of employers and
employed; they are essentially matters for individual dealing,
and not as a rule suitable for management by boards of
conciliation, which often have to deal with very wide areas.

Speaking generally then boards of conciliation have
nothing to do with the profits of particular employers.[6] But
they are very much concerned with the profits of employers
taken as a body : for these are the chief measures of the
prosperity and adversity of the trade; and in some cases
where the relations on both sides are thoroughly confidential,
it may be possible to explain to the employed the general
course of profits. Often, however, all that can be done is to
enable actuaries appointed by them to examine the books of
the firms concerned, and to ascertain from them the mean
prices got for the goods sold,[7] and in some cases a few other
broad facts; holding the rest of the knowledge thus acquired
under the oath of secrecy. These results are communicated
by them to the board, and are made the basis of the adjustment of wages; because they indicate better than any others
which are equally definite and easy of access, the amount of
the common net fund available for division between employers
and employed.

If the arrangement agreed on at any meeting is intended
to last only for a short time, and to be revised as soon as
there is any change in the circumstances of the trade, its
details may be handled with great freedom; many of them

---

may be determined in some measure by general impressions; they need not be calculated by rigid arithmetical processes from definite numerical data. Account may be taken of special circumstances which press heavily on employers or employed, or any group of them. In particular when irregular employment and low wages have caused much suffering among the employed and their families, the employers may be willing to trench on their reserve funds, and allow for a time wages to stand in such a relation to prices as would, if adopted as the basis of a permanent arrangement, soon land them in bankruptcy. If the meetings are frequent, and managed with frankness and kindliness, the future, though unknown, may cause no anxiety; it is nearly as good for either side to know that a fair concession will be made by the other whenever circumstances require it, as to know what that change will be. And the elasticity of this plan gives it great advantages over the rival plan of a " sliding scale;" that is a scale which determines beforehand how great a rise or fall in wages is to be accepted as the result of any given movement of prices upwards or downwards.

These advantages are of great importance in the case of a board which represents only a small area; for then frequent meetings involve no great expense or loss of time; the delegates can quickly ascertain the views of those whom they represent on any new turn of the situation. But if the area represented by a board is very wide, it must proceed on general rules; the delegates may be authorised to act frankly and fairly, but seldom to act generously, and therefore the elasticity gained by frequent meetings of the board will not be of much avail. For the settlement, then, of a price list for a wide area, a well thought out sliding scale seems to be the best means attainable under our present social conditions.

Studies such as those of Professor Munro and Mr. Price will help much towards a clear understanding of the principles on which sliding scales should be arranged. In some trades, as for instance in coal mining, there is very little outlay for

raw material, the circulating capital of the employers goes
almost wholly in wages, and the price of the product is the
best simple index of the prosperity of the trade. The plan
therefore of fixing wages in the coal trade at a fixed sum
together with a certain percentage of the price of coal is both
usual and satisfactory.[3] The profits or net receipts of the
employers of course oscillate more violently than their gross
receipts; and as these vary, as a rule, roughly with the price
of coal, this plan secures, as it should, that wages should
generally rise when profits rise, and fall when profits fall;
but with oscillations of less amplitude, rising less when they
rise, and falling less when they fall than profits do. In the
iron trade the cost of raw materials is heavy: and probably
the best simple scale for it is based on the excess of the
price of a ton of iron of a certain quality over the sums of
the prices of the coal and ironstone used in making it. As
however these latter prices are often subject to very much
the same influences as that of iron, the plan of basing the
scale on the price of iron simply seems not to work badly.
But in the textile and some other trades the prices of the
raw material depend on a great variety of causes (such as
the weather in America or Australia), and the standard must
be, not the price of the finished material, but the excess
of that over the price of the raw material of which it is
made.

Next money is a bad measure in which to express any
arrangement that is intended to last long: because the
purchasing power of money is always changing. When
trade is good and prices are high, the employer's fixed
charges are light, and he borrows with a light heart: when
trade is bad the consequent fall of prices increases the
burden of his fixed charges, and if called on to repay his
debt he must make very great sacrifices of his goods. A
perfect standard of purchasing power is unthinkable: even
a nearly perfect standard is unattainable. But government
could easily publish from time to time the money value of a

³ See p. 95.

unit of purchasing power which would be far more nearly constant than the value of money is.[9]

I think it ought to do that. And then nearly all wage arrangements, but especially all sliding scales, should be based on that unit. This would by one stroke make both wages and profits more stable, and at the same time increase the steadiness of employment. It would perhaps be a further improvement if a special unit could be made for wages : that should be based on the general unit, but differ from it by giving greater weight to the prices of the commodities chiefly used by the working classes. Details of this kind might, however, be arranged gradually and

---

[9] Government already does work of the kind desired in regard to the tithe commutation tables. But instead of dealing with wheat, barley, and oats, it would deal with all important commodities. It would publish their prices once a month or once a year ; it would reckon the importance of each commodity as proportioned to the total sum spent on it; and then by simple arithmetic deduce the change in the purchasing power of gold. Employers could arrange to pay as wages, instead of a fixed sum of (say) 30s., a sum of money so varying that it always gave the wage receiver the same purchasing power as 30s. did at the time of making the arrangement. Borrowings again could, at the option of the contracting parties, be reckoned in government units. On this plan, if A lends B 1,000l. at 4½ per cent. interest, and after some years the purchasing power of money had risen by an eighth, he would have to pay as interest, not 45l., but a sum that had the same purchasing power as 45l. had at the time of borrowing, i.e., 40l., and so on. The plan would have to win its way into general use ; but when it had once become familiar, none but gamblers would lend or borrow on any other terms, at all events for long periods. The scheme has no claims to theoretic perfection, but only to being a great improve. ment on our present methods attainable with little trouble. Even the rough results got by adding together (as the "Economist" does) the rise or fall in the wholesale prices of each of several important commodities, and taking the average of them, would provide a standard many times more stable than can be given by gold or silver, or even a combination of the two. But we might at once go a good deal beyond this, and gradually, as the machinery of our statistical departments improved, we might get very near to our ultimate aim—which is to obtain a unit (for the United Kingdom) which will give a uniform power of satisfying his wants to the average consumer ; that is to a person who consumes a 37,000,000th part of the total of every commodity consumed by the 37,000,000 inhabitants of the country. (See an article by the present writer in the "Contem- "porary Review" for March, 1887 ; also Jevons's "Money," chap. xxv.)

tentatively; and in fact this part of the work would probably best be done not by the government, but by boards of conciliation making use of the data supplied by government, and taking account of conditions special to their trade and locality.

So far we have supposed everything to work with perfect smoothness: but even when there is the best intention on either side of a board of conciliation to be frank, and to look at things as much as possible from the point of view of the other side, there must sometimes be differences of opinion which cannot be removed by discussion. A stage must sometimes be arrived at when further explanations seem to be worse than waste of time, and do but accentuate a deep seated difference of opinion. Therefore provision must always be made for referring some points to an independent arbitrator.[10] But here is a dilemma. If he is connected with the trade he is likely, even though he has no personal interest in the questions at issue, to enter on them with a certain bias: if he knows nothing of the trade, a great deal of time will be taken up in explaining to him the position, and after all he may not understand it rightly.[11] There has been much discussion as to which of these two evils is the greater. I venture to think that when there is mutual confidence and good temper, and when the suspicion of partisan bias is not likely to be strong, it is best to have an arbiter who already understands the trade, and can give his decision more promptly and more in detail than an outsider could. But when angry and jealous feelings have already been roused, when there is already a tendency on either side to impute unfairness to its opponents, then it is more important to know that the arbiter comes to the question without bias, than that he will understand it quickly, and be able to enter into all its details.

The action of the arbitrator must in some respects depend on the temper in which the case is presented to him. Sometimes the true facts of the case will be put

[10] See p. 39. [11] See pp. 49—53.

before him at once, neither side making *ex parte* statements; and, what is even more important, neither side so mistrusting the other as to refuse to make concessions lest they should be taken to indicate weakness and fear, and encourage the other side to be the more aggressive. Sometimes also he will be given to understand that he should determine what is fair with reference only to the general tendency of economic forces, and that he is not to take account of the extent of the preparations for war ready on either side. In other cases, in which hostile feelings are already roused, the leaders may be unable to guarantee that the rank and file will accept a decision that awards them much worse terms than they could get for themselves by a sharp strike or lock-out. The arbitrator then is compelled to take some account of the fighting forces of the two sides; the necessity to be practical may compel him to go further than he would otherwise have done, away from an absolute standard of fairness. In such cases, too, he must take for granted that the statements made by either side will be *ex parte*, and conduct his inquiry more or less after the manner of the law courts. This method of investigation is so cumbrous and slow that it cannot be very often resorted to; but if it does its work thoroughly in a typical case, the indirect influence of its final award may extend very far: it may help many other differences to be settled quickly and quietly in private conversation or by boards of conciliation, and thus may be well worth the time and trouble it requires.

When a board of conciliation meets in angry temper, and it is certain from the beginning that the questions at issue must be fought out before an arbiter, the procedure, though technically different, is practically the same as in the plan which usually goes by the name of arbitration. It may be convenient sometimes to contrast sharply the two methods of conciliation and arbitration, but Mr. Price seems to be right in treating them together, and regarding them as two forms of the same thing. Arbitration technically so called must begin with a more or less conciliatory meeting of delegates to agree on an arbiter, and draw out a case to be submitted to him; and the principles on which he has to act are generally the same as they would have been if the case were put before him by a board of conciliation in an angry mood.

An arbiter, even if he starts with a knowledge of the trade, cannot deal with a detailed price list as easily as a board of conciliation, in which there is a healthy spirit, and which can appoint sub-committees to draw up the first drafts of portions of the price lists relating to special branches of the trade. Therefore when there is a great variety of detail, any other course than that of conciliation seems hopeless; there is little room even for the action of trades unions, except in the matter of accustoming the workers to know and trust one another, to select able delegates, and to submit bravely to their decision.[12] But this is a most important exception: independently of any direct effect on wages, trades unions have done an inestimable service by teaching members of the same trade to know and trust one another, to act together, and to discuss under the guidance of the ablest minds among them questions of wide and far-seeing policy.

In this connection it becomes very important to know how far the working classes are migratory in their habits. Mr. Ravenstein has recently found that they are much more migratory than is generally supposed; and the study of this question with which Mr. Price ends his essay,[13] is an important contribution to the data of economics.

It has been suggested that boards of conciliation may lead employers and employed to set themselves to exclude competition, even perhaps to resist improvements in production that would diminish their own employment, and in short to follow the example set them by many mediæval guilds, of hardening themselves into organised conspiracies for promoting the well being of the privileged few at the expense of the great mass of the people. But thanks to the publicity of

[12] See pp. 104 and 105.   [13] See pp. 106, &c.

modern times, to the rapid migration of industries, and to the keenness of foreign competition in most trades, there is very little fear of this great evil. There is more danger that improvements in the organisation of some classes of workers may lead to the oppression of other classes who are joined with them in the same production, but are not organised;[14] and thus in all economic questions considerations of the higher ethics will always assert themselves, however much we try to limit our inquiry for an immediate practical purpose. Conciliation is helpless to secure for the feeblest and most ignorant class of workers a decent wage. The " sweater," who, as some sweaters do, works hard himself, earns but a moderate income, and pays promptly and ungrudgingly the highest wages that the trade will bear, cannot be said to act unfairly; but yet few are bold enough to say that he pays fair wages. The fact is that the root of this difficulty is not so much in our methods of business, as in those of education in the broadest sense of the term. Production is at fault, but it is the production of human beings. The fundamental wrong is in allowing large classes of people to grow up with so poor an education, physical, mental, and moral, that they are unfit for intelligent and energetic work, and must crowd into and pull down the wages of the few kinds of work of which they are capable. For this evil the ultimate remedy is in the higher education of the mass of the people. School work is useful as a foundation: but by itself it reaches only a little way. Trades unions have increased the intelligence of the workman, by opening his mind to broader problems; boards of conciliation, together with the great co-operative movement, are carrying his education further. They are giving him an acquaintance with the real problems of business, which is the one thing wanted, provided he has good natural abilities, for enabling him to do the higher work of organising the world's production. Every increase in the ranks of those who have this power, increases the competition of employers

[14] See for instance the case of the platers and their helpers, p. 15.

for the aid of the employed, and diminishes the toll which has to be paid by the working classes to those who organise the work of the community. And further, anything that widens the intelligence of working men of ordinary ability, who have no natural capacity for the highest work, improves the prevailing tone with regard to the manner of expending the family income, and the responsibilities of parents towards their children.

Conciliation is thus a powerful means of raising the working classes: it is scarcely less powerful a means of raising their employers. The frank and free intercourse at the boards is helping employers to look at their business on its human side, to see that sometimes what is little more than a mere move in a game to them, may affect the whole future of many families; may help happy lives to expand in full vigour, or may turn them into a sour and stunted feebleness. The knowledge and sympathy thus gained by the employers raise those even of the rich who are not in business, widen their notions of justice, and aid them in realising the responsibilities of wealth.

All these are steps upwards: they have not the rapid pace of a revolution: but a revolution generally rushes backwards faster and further than it had moved forwards; and steps such as these move steadily onwards.

ALFRED MARSHALL.

28th June, 1887.

NOTE BY THE AUTHOR.

The material for this report was collected in the spring of 1886, during a residence of some fifteen weeks in the city of Newcastle-upon-Tyne; and the report itself was written during the summer of the same year. Some of the details, therefore, in the text may not be correct to date; and this is more especially the case with regard to the sliding scale in the Northumberland coal trade, which terminated last December, in accordance with a notice given by the employers.

It has been thought better, however, to leave the text as it was written, and to indicate in the notes the subsequent changes, so far as it has been possible to ascertain them. This has been done because it is difficult to obtain accurate data of minute details without actual residence in the industrial districts where those changes have taken place—and this has not been possible—and also because it is hoped that the conclusions which have been drawn from the facts collected in the report cannot have been as yet materially affected by subsequent events. Nor indeed can there be much doubt that after a period of time—which may be brief or may unhappily be long—the Northumberland masters and men will return to the system of arranging wages by a sliding scale.

The subject of the migration of labour may perhaps appear to have been discussed at disproportionate length. But the point is at present involved in such obscurity that it is difficult to deal with it at all without being led on to a lengthy treatment, and the discussion—inadequate as it is—will, it is hoped, serve to illustrate and support the main contention of the report.

The number of references contained in the notes is, it is feared, abnormally great; but an endeavour has been made to supply them in each instance in order to show that—so far as it has proved to be possible—the statements in the report are based upon actual fact.

The author's indebtedness to those who have kindly furnished him with information upon the several points discussed will be found for the most part, it is hoped, to be acknowledged in the notes. But to the names specially mentioned a number of friends must be added, who most readily gave their assistance, and whose spontaneous kindness will always cause him to associate the most pleasant recollections with his residence on Tyneside. To Professor Marshall, for lending to the report the honourable distinction of a preface from his pen, the author feels that he cannot better express his gratitude than by saying that it is only one out of the many acts of kindness which Professor Marshall has shown to a pupil who is conscious that he owes to his teaching at Oxford the first practical guidance in economic study.

ORIEL COLLEGE, OXFORD,
    4th May, 1887.

CONTENTS.

CHAPTER IV.

THE THIRD STAGE: THE ESTABLISHMENT OF SLIDING SCALES.

CHAPTER V.

INDUSTRIAL CIRCUMSTANCES FAVOURING PEACE.

INDUSTRIAL PEACE:

ITS

ADVANTAGES, METHODS, AND DIFFICULTIES.

CHAPTER I.

INTRODUCTORY MATTER.

IF there is one fact more than another which seems to be forced home upon the mind of the inquirer by the study of industrial and economic problems, it is this—that there is not, nor indeed is it probable that there can be, any single panacea for social ills. But the recognition of this fact, paradoxical as the inference may at first sight appear, really supplies no adequate warrant for any deadening or pessimistic despondency as to the prospects of the future improvement of society, but is rather the necessary condition of a healthy and sturdy optimism. For so seldom is it really the case, in the economic sphere of things at least, that history exactly "repeats itself," and so diversified are the details of even contemporaneous industrial society, that any scheme which professes to cure all economic maladies by an uniform unalterable method of treatment may almost be said to carry with it its own condemnation. And were we to rest all our hopes of the improvement of society upon any one of the many panaceas which are prescribed from time to time by ardent enthusiasts, whose ardour perhaps is more conspicuous than their discretion; were all our "ventures" "in one "bottom trusted," then indeed the prospect might well be gloomy enough to call for the most despairing pessimism, for then to the success or failure of a single scheme would be linked, for better or for worse, the fortunes of society. The significance, however, of this fact is often neglected. Again and again the world is told, and the tale has been reiterated so often that it now falls, in some cases, we are afraid, upon deaf or unwilling, in others upon disappointed and incredulous ears, that a "simple yet sovereign "remedy" for social ills has been found—a remedy of universal

B

application, and a remedy of undoubted and indubitable efficacy. And on the other hand, again and again is the kindred fallacy committed of arguing from the failure or success of a remedy in a particular case, to its necessary failure or success in all cases and under all conditions.

"Co-operation," for example, it has been strenuously urged, "is destined to heal all our industrial sores. Let it only be applied "to the production of wealth as it has been to its distribution, and "we shall see no more the glaring contrast between rich and poor, "which is so striking a feature of modern society, nor shall we "hear any longer of those disastrous conflicts between capital and "labour which are now apparently chronic affections of our indus- "trial system, for capital and labour will be harmoniously united "in the same persons." But upon this point the experience of the past has not been very encouraging. Distributive co-operation, indeed, or, more correctly speaking, "consumptive co-operation," can point to a record of brilliant and rapid progress—so rapid, that Mr. Gladstone[1] once described it in the House of Commons as a " social marvel"—but co-operative production, in striking comparison with this, has scarcely made any real advance. An estimate[2] of its extent in England made at the beginning of the year 1884 showed that only 800,000l. of capital were employed in this direction ; that the value of the annual production was 3,080,000l., and the number of employees 6,300 ; and these figures, we must remember, included not a few associations which did not carry the co-operative principle so far as to give a bonus upon labour. A more exact analysis, too, of industrial society has revealed fresh difficulties in its path. The essential object at which it aims has been shown to be, not the union of capital and labour in the same persons, but the far more serious matter of " getting rid of the employer," to use Professor Walker's[3] instruc- tive phrase ; and so, in proportion to the magnitude of the work he performs in modern industry, must be the difficulty experienced in discovering any effectual substitute for him in the way of co- operative production.

A system, however, of "industrial partnership" or "profit-

---

[1] Cf. in 1864. Cf. "Working Men Co-operators," by A. H. D. Acland and B. Jones, p. 20, foot note.
[2] Cf. op. cit., p. 102. Cf. also the report of a committee on productive and distributive co-operation to the Co-operative Congress, published in the Report of the Seventeenth Annual Co-operative Congress (1885), pp. 9 and 78—116. The committee say, " that as a committee we are agreed that the time is not ripe for "general work." The report, however, it must be said, gave rise to a heated discussion, pp. 9—11.
[3] Cf. "The Wages Question," by F. A. Walker, ch. xv, p. 265 (edition 1884), and also " Economics of Industry," by A. and M. P. Marshall, iii, ix, 4.

"sharing" seems to meet these specific difficulties; for by this scheme the benefit of the interested and experienced management of the employer is secured, together with that of the interested and organised labour of the workmen. But it would be rash to conclude that even this system is likely to be universally adopted. It is more reasonable and more in accordance with the experience of the past to look for the development of industrial reform in various directions, and to expect diversity rather than uniformity of method.

Thus, despite of the difficulties which have to be met, we may hope to see in the future many varieties of co-operative production put into practice. We need not be disheartened by such a failure as that of the Ouseburn Engine Works in Newcastle[4]—conspicuous and disastrous as it was, and prejudicial as it has been to the cause of co-operative production in the north. For, if zeal be but tempered with discretion, if the experience of the past be used to impress the necessity of precautions against special dangers and peculiar difficulties, if progress be made slowly but surely, if a favourable sphere of action be chosen where the difficulties of management are small and the fluctuations of trade reduced to a minimum, where the enthusiasm of the workers is effectually kindled, and their knowledge of the conditions of successful business extended, then co-operative production may attain success —and marked success—on a large scale ; and on a small scale the principle may be applied in various degrees and according to various methods.[5] The system of industrial partnership, again, is full of promise for the future ; and it is the more promising because it seems to possess in a high degree the quality of elasticity, and to be capable of ready adaptation to different circumstances.

But we may still expect to see the old relation of wage-payer and wage-receiver continuing side by side with these new developments. There is a great deal of truth in the contention of M. Leroy-Beaulieu,[6] that profit-sharing does not do away with wages, but is rather supplementary to them, and that the profits thus shared are to wages what salt and pepper, oil and vinegar, are to bread and meat—a kind of relish which imparts a savour to food, and renders it healthier and more agreeable, but does not of itself constitute food. And there is a capriciousness about the spread, even of co-operative distribution, in England which is very suggestive. Mr. Thomas

---

[4] "Lectures on the Labour Question," by T. Brassey, pp. 131—133.

[5] E.g , in the form of contracts or sub-contracts, as under the system of "Tut-work" and "Tribute" in the Cornish mines.

[6] Cf. "Essai sur la répartition des richesses," par P. Leroy-Beaulieu. Deuxième édition, p. 370.

Hughes,[1] when seconding a vote of thanks to Mr. Lloyd Jones for his presidential address at the Co-operative Congress of 1885, compared the position of Oldham, the town where the Congress was sitting, with that of Birmingham,—"the centre," as he said, "of industrial radical reform," with "the centre of political "reform"—and pointed out that the latter "had no co-operative "society until three years ago," and that it now "only numbered "1,500 members," while Oldham could set its "thousands of "co-operators." against the "twenties" of Birmingham. Some tables[3] appended to the report of the Congress illustrated this point, and showed that the north-western section could point to a membership of 376,234 in the year 1884, and to a list of societies amounting to 437, while the midland section had only 196 societies and 68,394 members. And yet co-operative distribution does not seem to be a very recondite principle, or one which is very difficult to put into practice.

If then we may, for a considerable time at least—so long indeed that it is difficult, if not impossible, as yet to see clearly beyond this point—expect the existing relation of wage-payer and wage-receiver to survive, it is of the highest importance to examine the methods by which that relation may be made more harmonious and the danger of friction reduced. And, even if we might hope with any reason for a rapid extension of co-operative production or a speedy development of industrial partnership, the examination would not on that account lose its value. For it does not seem to be by any means certain that either the one or the other of these two systems will entirely remove all occasion for industrial conflict, though they may render it very improbable. Lord Brassey[9] has drawn attention to the occurrence of a strike in the Ouseburn Co-operative Engine Works, and the incident, despite of the peculiar circumstances of that unfortunate undertaking, is of no little significance. Nor would it be difficult to show from a theoretical standpoint, that there are many possibilities of friction in the working of co-operative production or industrial partnership; and the disputants may, not inconceivably, avail themselves of the habitual weapons of industrial warfare. The proportion of the bonus to be paid out of profits to wages earned or work done under a system of industrial partnership, and the relative position of the different classes of workers in this respect—if there is to be any attempt to reward special assiduity or extraordinary skill—the choice of a manager, and the decisions of committees of direction

---

[1] *Cf.* Co-operative Congress Report, p. 7.

[8] *Cf. op. cit.*, p. 147. The northern section with 138 societies showed a membership of 105,521. *Cf.* also "Working Men Co-operators," p. 31.

[9] *Cf.* "Lectures on the Labour Question," p. 131.

in co-operative production, must, so long as human nature remains unaltered in its main characteristics, present occasions of possible difference of opinion, and may not improbably be used as a *casus belli* by the dissatisfied party.

In examining the special question of the peaceful settlement of industrial disputes, we must never lose sight of these general considerations. For here, as elsewhere, we must not expect to find that there is one uniform method which can be applied with certainty of success to all industries and to every dispute, but we must rather be prepared to recognise the greatest diversity of detail. It is because the principle of conciliation is capable of the most varied application, and can, while it remains unaltered as a principle, be readily adapted and modified in its details so as to suit the different circumstances of different industries, that Mr. Crompton, in his essay on "Industrial Conciliation,"[10] has claimed for it the title of a "panacea." It is not rigid and inflexible, but is, on the contrary, as ductile and plastic as could well be desired.

And yet we must not forget that, just as it seems fanciful to expect that a time will ever come in this dispensation, when throughout the length and breadth of the world swords will be turned into plough-shares and spears into pruning-hooks, and just as it needed a poet's imagination to discern

"The Vision of the world, and all the wonder that would be;"

and to look further and further into the future,

"Till the war-drum throbb'd no longer, and the battle-flags were furl'd
In the Parliament of man, the Federation of the world."—

So too in the industrial sphere, he would be a rash prophet who would predict an entire cessation of conflict, and would therefore erase the words "strike" and "lock-out" from his economic vocabulary. What we have to remember is that it is something gained to diminish the frequency and to mitigate the bitterness of these conflicts, though it would be better—were it possible—to dispense with them altogether, just as it is something gained, as we shall have occasion to notice, to procure a peaceful settlement of industrial disputes, when once they have come to an open quarrel, by means of negotiation or arbitration, though it would be better to entirely prevent the quarrel by previous conciliation. Mr. Bevan, indeed, in a paper[11] read before the Statistical Society of London, and published in the March number of its *Journal* for 1880, drew

---

[10] "Industrial Conciliation," by H. Crompton, p. 10.

[11] Statistical Society's *Journal*, vol. xliii, March, 1880, "The Strikes of the "Past Ten Years," by G. P. Bevan.

up a catalogue of the strikes which had occurred—so far as any tolerably accurate chronicle could be obtained—in the years 1870-79, and arrived at a grand total of 2,352. Hence he concluded that strikes were chronic diseases of our industrial constitution, and that the " success of arbitration " had been " far too doubtful " for it to be regarded as an effectual remedy. And, in the discussion which followed, Mr. Bunning, who has had a very considerable experience in the peaceful settlement of industrial disputes,[12] stated that he " did not think that " in the " nature of things," " strikes " would ever cease."

But there are, on the other hand, several encouraging facts to be noticed in the history and the working of the many various methods which may perhaps be correctly embraced under the one generic name of " industrial conciliation." It is at least certain that no little amount of the barbarity which accompanied the strikes of the early part of this century—barbarity not perhaps wholly unnatural considering the circumstances of the times, and the anomalies of the laws, though none the less deserving of the sternest condemnation—has now passed away ; and, if the ultimate appeal is made to force, it is not, as a general rule, before reason has been invoked ; nor are the disputants on either side entirely deaf to reason when the struggle of force has once commenced. We hear even now, and we must expect to hear, of isolated cases of unmanly intimidation. We sometimes see, even in England, an outburst of passionate violence, when the safety of property is menaced and the security of person endangered. But these outbursts are very occasional ; and it may be fairly said that—despite of such indications as the satisfaction expressed by the silk manufacturers[13] of Macclesfield before the Royal Commission on the Depression of Trade at the decline or even disappearance of trades unions from their town—there is a growing consensus of opinion that the legal recognition of trades unions has run side by side with the disuse of illegal practices, and that the growth of organisation is almost coincident with increasing willingness to listen to reasonable argument.

We noticed before that the peaceful settlement of industrial disputes might be effected in various ways, and proceed on different lines. In one case there may be no organised system

---

[12] In connection with the coal trades of Northumberland and Durham, as secretary of the " Steam Collieries' Defence Association," and also of the " Durham " Coal Owners' Association." Mr. Bunning added that their number could be, he thought, " much diminished."

[13] Cf. Report of the Royal Commission appointed to inquire into the Depression of Trade and Industry. Q. 7239—42, 7394, and 7493. Despite of the disappearance of unions from Macclesfield, a strike seems to have occurred in April, 1886. Q. 13831—4.

for the settlement of disputes, but merely occasional and irregular negotiations between the two parties, either before the open declaration of conflict or during the continuance of the struggle; and the question in dispute may sometimes be referred to the decision of an arbitrator. In another case there may be an organised machinery for the prevention of disputes and the harmonious adjustment of points of difference. There may be, in short, established boards of conciliation or courts of arbitration. These boards, again, may vary in their constitution and action. They may settle the industrial relations of the future as well as the quarrels of the past; and they may for this end adopt different lines of conduct. They may from time to time arrive at definite agreements as to the rate of wages; or they may construct a "sliding scale," as it is called, by which wages may almost be said to regulate themselves automatically in accordance with fluctuations in price or some other standard. Nor is one principle only employed in the construction of these scales.

It would be absurd, therefore, to pretend that there is any regular law of development in the peaceful settlement of industrial disputes. For the varieties we have mentioned above are not mutually exclusive. We may distinguish arbitration from conciliation on the ground that the one is chiefly applicable to the settlement of disputes as to the past, and the other to the arrangement of industrial relations for the future, or on the more solid ground that the latter is voluntary and the former compulsory in character. But in making this distinction we must remember that provision for arbitration is often, nay generally, made in the constitution of boards of conciliation, and that it is employed to settle the rate of wages for the future as well as to adjust the quarrels of the past. Nor, as we shall see hereafter, does the "automatic" regulation of wages by a sliding scale exclude the occasional intervention of arbitration or conciliation; for a common ground of action must be agreed upon at starting, and modifications may from time to time be necessitated by fluctuations in trade, which were not contemplated at the first construction of the scale. To lay down, then, a definite order of succession in which one method of the settlement of disputes is and must be developed from another, would be as open to objection as it would be for philologists to suppose that in all cases languages have passed from a monosyllabic to an agglutinative, and from that again to an inflexional stage; or for students of sociology to maintain that all races of men have gone through the various steps of development put forward by different theories of primitive society.[11] If there

---

[11] E.g., the writings of Morgan and McLennan.

are differences between different industries, then a method of conciliation suited to the circumstances of one may conflict with the traditions and unwritten law of another; and here, if anywhere, it seems necessary to clearly recognise the fact that, if the principle is to work smoothly, the details must be left for settlement in each case to the interested parties.

But though it would be impossible and irrational to lay down a necessary historical order of development, it will be convenient, as it has been found to be in analogous cases, to construct a theoretical order, and to endeavour to group our consideration of the different varieties of conciliation round some central points. We may then distinguish, roughly and hypothetically, three stages of development; one, where there is no organised machinery for the settlement of disputes, but merely occasional and irregular negotiation; another, where there is an organised machinery, but wages are settled periodically by definite arrangement; and a third, where wages are regulated automatically by a sliding scale. We must remember of course that these stages overlap one another, and that the distinction between them is arbitrary. But with this proviso, we may take for a typical instance of the first stage the negotiations in a recent strike in the shipbuilding industry on the banks of the Tyne and the Wear. For the second stage we may select the board of conciliation and arbitration in the manufactured iron trade of the north of England; and for the third and last stage, the sliding scales in operation in the coal trades of Northumberland and Durham. I have chosen these three instances because I have had special opportunity of acquiring information about them. But they are also very instructive for our purpose, as they are all connected with the same industrial district, and yet exhibit very considerable differences with regard to the question under discussion.

CHAPTER II.

THE FIRST STAGE IN THE THEORETICAL ORDER OF DEVELOPMENT: IRREGULAR NEGOTIATIONS.

(A). First, then, let us take the case of the shipbuilding strike upon the Tyne and the Wear. Into the details of the question under dispute and the merits of the contentions put forward by the opposing parties, it is not relevant to our present purpose to enter. What we are concerned with is the course of the negotiations which resulted in a final settlement of the quarrel.

At the close of the year 1885, according to the monthly report issued for March, 1886,[15] by the general secretary to the United Society of Boilermakers and Iron Shipbuilders, the shipbuilders throughout the whole of the north-east coast of England gave notice of a " very heavy reduction " in wages applying to all the members of the society in their employment. This reduction affected directly, or indirectly, " more than 8,000 " members of the society, and was the fourth which had taken place within two years. A strike thereupon followed, but during the month of January the men opened negotiations with the masters and submitted a proposal, which was however rejected.

Towards the end of the month, again, rumours began to spread of fresh negotiations. It is worthy of notice in passing, that inasmuch as the district had not as yet been formally put upon the "strike allowance," as it is termed, by the council of the society, the negotiations for the settlement of the dispute rested entirely with the workmen immediately concerned, and the council could only act "upon special invitation" instead of taking complete control over the matter, as it would have done supposing the district had already been receiving " strike allowance."[16] The men, indeed, were apparently beginning to suffer "considerable" pecuniary distress, and their committee issued a circular appealing for " sympathy and support " to the various trade-societies in the

---

[15] Cf. "Newcastle Daily Chronicle," 19th March, 1886.
[16] Cf. "Newcastle Daily Chronicle, " 1st February, 1886; "Newcastle Daily " Leader," 1st February, 1886.

district. In this circular they were careful to draw special attention
to the fact that they had offered a proposal for the settlement of the
dispute to the employers before making any appeal for pecuniary
aid.[17] A mass meeting of men representing the different lodges of
the society on Tyne-side, and numbering some 700 or 800, was
held at Wallsend on the 1st of February;[18] and, though the proceedings were private, it was generally understood that the whole
question of the reduction of wages was thoroughly discussed.
On 5th February[19] a meeting of the Tyne and Wear shipbuilders
was held at Sunderland, and a deputation from the Boilermakers' Society—comprising four representatives from the Tyne
and four from the Wear, together with two "delegates"—
was present. The views of the opposing parties were inter-
changed and their relative position explained. The deputation
then withdrew, and on being readmitted was informed that the
employers were "prepared to take into favourable consideration
" any modification which the men" might "propose of the reduc-
" tion already notified." A strong recommendation was offered to
the effect that deputations of the men should be invested with full
powers to treat for a final settlement of the dispute, and an
arrangement was made for a meeting on the following Thursday to
receive the reply to the proposal of the employers. The
deputation met that evening and discussed the position of affairs,
and a Newcastle paper[20] of the next day reported that a proposal
was about to be submitted to the various districts which might
bring about a solution of the difficulty. On Saturday, the 6th of
February, the first distribution of "strike-money" took place at
Sunderland at the different lodges; for the executive of the society
had granted a sum of 5,000l. for that purpose to be distributed in
weekly allowances of 8s. a man.[21] On 10th February, the evening
before the adjourned meeting of the employers, a meeting of the
representatives of the men was held, when the returns from the
various lodges with reference to the proposal of the employers
were received.[22] The next day the masters met the deputation
from the Boilermakers' Society, and were informed[23] that not only
were the votes of the men opposed to any reduction, but that they
also refused to give the deputation powers of negotiation. The
employers expressed their "surprise and regret" at a course of
action which "virtually closed the door to negotiation;" but,
after a private discussion, they themselves offered the men a
modification in the proposed reduction, reminding them, through
the mouth of their chairman, that for their part they had adopted

[17] Cf. op. cit.   [18] Ibid, 2nd February, 1886.
[19] Ibid., 6th February.   [20] Cf. op. cit.   [21] Cf. op cit., 8th February.
[22] Ibid., 11th February.   [23] Ibid., 12th February.

a "conciliatory attitude" throughout the dispute, that they had asked the representatives of the men "to meet them in friendly "conference" prior to the issue of the notice, and that they had requested them to send a deputation to a meeting even after the men had passed a resolution against the acceptance of "any "reduction whatever." The employers' proposal was again submitted in the usual way to the various lodges; and it seems that, while some of the lodges were opposed to any reduction, others—and more especially those on the Wear—were anxious to come to terms.[21] On the 18th the masters again met the representatives of the men, who submitted a proposal for a reduction indeed, but not of the same amount as that demanded by the masters. A long discussion ensued, and ultimately the masters, without accepting the proposal, made a further modification in their terms.[25] Finally, after some further negotiation, the dispute was settled about the end of the month.

B (i). The history of this dispute is not without its hopeful signs, although we cannot but echo the words of Mr. Knight, the general secretary of the Boilermakers' Society, when he states, in his monthly report for March, that it was "a pity that the compromise "was not come to before these weeks were spent in idleness."[26] What we have to remember is that it is something gained to mitigate the bitterness of these conflicts; and there can be no doubt that, if a comparison were instituted between the history of such a strike as this, and the history of the strikes of some thirty or forty, perhaps even some ten or twenty years ago, there would be abundant evidence to prove that a considerable change had taken place in the nature of these conflicts, and that many of their old barbarous accessories had passed away. Mr. Knight himself remarks in the report to which previous reference has been made, that "of this strike or lock-out, or whatever it may be called, it "must be said that it has been conducted in the most excellent "spirit possible on both sides. There has been little recrimination. "There has been no violence."

Nor is this statement by any means exaggerated. From both sides we have an expression of reluctance at the occurrence of the dispute. To quote Mr. Knight again, he states that "these "violent stoppages may be necessary, but they are the wars of "the industrial world, and should never be lightly resorted to." And, in his annual report for 1885,[27] he notices the fact, that

---

[21] *Cf.* "Newcastle Daily Chronicle," 18th February.
[25] *Cf.* "Newcastle Daily Leader," 19th February.
[26] *Cf.* "Newcastle Daily Chronicle," 19th March.
[27] *Cf.* Annual Report for 1885 of the United Society of Boilermakers and Iron Shipbuilders, p. xi.

3,593*l.* has been spent during the year on disputes, and, while declaring that " these civil wars are necessary evils sometimes," he adds, " we are always favourable to peace with honour." On the part of the masters we have the statement made by their chairman at the meeting of 11th February, to which reference has already been made, and throughout the course of the negotiations they again and again express a desire to arrive at a peaceful settlement.

On both sides again there is evidence of a wish to be accurate in the statements made and the contentions put forward. During the continuance of the dispute a letter appeared from Mr. Knight in the " Newcastle Daily Leader " of 17th February, with reference to an extract from his monthly report for February, which had been published in that paper, and contained an assertion which he had since discovered to be incomplete, and therefore to reflect unfairly upon the conduct of the managers of a certain ship-building firm. In this letter he asks to be allowed to supplement the former statement, " as," he says, " we should be very sorry to say anything, or make a partial statement, that might in the " slightest degree reflect unjustly on the officials of the firm at " Elswick." The masters in like manner are reported by the " New-" castle Daily Leader " of 19th February to have expressed a willingness, at a meeting of masters and representative men, " to " allow any chartered accountants, mutually agreed on, to inspect " their wages-books and verify " the " averages " which they had put forward at a similar meeting on the 11th.

(ii). Of course in all such disputes we must expect to find irritation and friction on either side. The fact cannot be disguised that in such a dispute as this we have an industrial war; and it is because these contests, like wars, have an inevitable tendency to engender bitterness of feeling, and to stereotype an attitude of mutual hostility, that they are to be so deeply regretted. Mr. Knight's monthly report for March, to which we have so often referred before, supplies a very apt illustration of this point. In reading his account of the dispute, we cannot fail to be reminded again and again of the analogy between a strike and a war. We have, first, looking at the matter from his point of view, the formal declaration of war, in the notice of reduction issued by the employers. Then follows an estimate of the resources of either side. " The employers from the outset had circumstances considerably in " their favour, so far as *mere fighting* went. Work was not very " plentiful. The most important work was work that could wait, " and in the chief contracts strikes were provided for. The " stoppage to them caused little inconvenience, and when it was " over work would be all the brisker . . . . . . They had the

" strongest *battalions*, they had hunger on their side." Then
he examines the position of his own side. " The members, on the
" other hand, had all the prevailing circumstances against them.
" An exceedingly large number are without employment of any sort.
" Many families are without food. The season has been painfully
" severe, and all funds available for support have been strained to
" the utmost." And then after remarking that " it was inevitable
" that there should be a compromise in the end, unless the men
" were to yield the whole," he states the essence of the matter in a
single sentence. " They have made a very *gallant stand*, looked at
" purely as a stand for better terms, and they have *won half the*
" *battle*."[28] Here then we have a description of an industrial war,
and we may expect to find evils somewhat analogous to the evils of
war resulting therefrom.

(*a*). Now it would be easy to draw up a lengthy catalogue of
the possible evils occasioned by these conflicts. It is a very common
practice to calculate on the one side the sum which these strikes
entail in the loss of wages during the stoppage of work, and on the
other the sum gained in the shape of an increase, or a prevention of
a reduction, of wages; to construct an imaginary balance sheet; to
prove incontestably that the former of these two sums is very much
larger than the other, and then to throw this in the teeth of the
workmen, and to point out in a manner forcible rather than
persuasive, the unmistakable error of their ways.

But such a balance sheet is very unsatisfactory. It is difficult
to arrive with even approximate accuracy, at an estimate of either
side of the account. To the loss of wages we have to add the
possibility of falling into debt, which it may take a lifetime to
redeem; the departure it may be of trade from the district, and as
a consequence of this, the permanent curtailment of employment;
and last, but by no means least, the abiding injury inflicted upon
body, mind, and character, by irregular habits, and, in all likelihood, irregular meals. On the other side of the account there
are moral considerations which do not admit of reduction to a
pecuniary standard, and a workman of the north of England once
remarked to me, that he thought that any of the privations he
might have endured during the famous Nine-hours' strike, were
abundantly compensated by the advantages of the increased
leisure and independence he had since enjoyed.

From a strictly economic point of view again, it is now
generally allowed that it is dangerous to conclude that a strike is
in all cases prejudicial even to the permanent economic interests
of the workmen. For the increased efficiency of labour due to

---

[28] The *italics* are my own.

better health, to better education, to better character, may conceivably compensate for the diminution of the working hours of a
day, or for increased wages, or for temporary stoppage of production; and the growth of that capital which is so necessary to
industry may depend upon the willingness to save, not merely of
employers—who indeed may conceivably habituate themselves to a
lower rate of interest and to smaller profits—but also of workmen,
who may find in their larger wages at once greater ability and
greater inducement to save. Here then also there are moral
elements which baffle exact calculation. The one thing which
does seem certain is this, that an industrial conflict, like a war
between nations, does leave behind feelings of bitterness, and does
by its very nature prevent the growth of harmonious and amicable
relations. These are certain calamities and indisputable evils.
And hence, if there is to be provision for war, it is eminently
desirable that there should also be provision for negotiation.

In this negotiation, indeed, we must expect to find some
irregularity of working, and to see some irritation displayed. For
we must remember that in such cases as that we have just
described, the negotiation is conducted between two disputants
who are actually engaged in a fray where vital interests are at
stake; who have probably not a little soreness of feeling towards
one another; who in all likelihood are suffering pecuniary injury
from the conflict, and who are not habituated, as they would be
were there a regular board of conciliation, or traditional method of
arbitration, recognised in the industry, to meet one another round
the same table, and to adjust their differences by formal argument
or mutual concession. There is, in fact, no common basis from
which to start; and the matter is rather to be settled by the
estimate which either side forms of the comparative strength of
its opponents and itself. Nor, be it noticed, does there seem to be
any economic standard which can be called into requisition in such
disputes, for as Professor Sidgwick[29] has pointed out, where two
combinations meet one another, political economy is perforce
silenced. Each side then is determined to secure all it can; each
side is naturally suspicious of the attitude of the other. The
hopeful sign is this, that the parties are willing to meet one
another, and that they are desirous of arriving at a settlement.

(b). And here we must in the last place notice a point to which
we shall again have to draw attention when we consider other
forms of conciliation. It is of little use for negotiations to be
commenced unless the negotiators are invested with plenipotentiary
authority, or are at any rate the accredited representatives of the

[29] Cf. "Principles of Political Economy," II, X, 1, p. 319, foot note;
2, p. 355.

opposing forces. In the shipbuilding strike which we have just examined, there was one fact of a very melancholy character which could not but impress itself forcibly upon the mind of the observer. The labourers in the shipbuilding yards, the "helpers" as they are commonly called, had no part or lot in the strike, and yet with the suspension of industry they were thrown out of employment. It need hardly be said that the resources on which they could fall back were far more slender than those of the skilled workmen. A system is in vogue, with few exceptions, in the yards on the Tyne and the Wear, by which the "platers," &c., are paid by the piece, and the "helpers" by the time.[30] And thus during the halcyon days of prosperity in the shipbuilding trade—and even in brisk times we must remember the average working days in a week do not seem to be more than four—the platers might earn high wages, and yet the helpers might derive little benefit. For the platers working by the piece, might stay away from the yards during some days of the week, trusting to make up for the time lost by extra-hard work upon the remaining days, but the helpers would lose their time-wages during the days when the platers were idle, and would have to take their share of the high pressure speed on the other days. An attempt was made some few years ago by a Mr. Lynch, who was himself at one time a labourer in the yards, to organise a union among "the helpers," and to obtain an alteration of the system; but the attempt had only a temporary success, partly, it seems, from the natural want of cohesion which is so characteristic of unskilled labourers, and partly also it is to be feared through the opposition of the members of the Boiler-makers' Society, and the importation of labourers from outside to take the places of the recalcitrant helpers.[31] And so, when the time of the strike came, the helpers were thrown out of employ-ment, with little, if any, resources to meet the distress by which they were confronted; and to add to the hardness of their position, they were apparently deemed ineligible for relief from the general distress fund set on foot during the winter in the city of New-castle, because they were regarded as concerned in the strike.[32] In one district, however, at least, they organised a committee, and appealed to the public for pecuniary aid. But the fact which is so forcibly impressed upon the mind is this, that during all the negotiations between the shipbuilders and the members of the Boilermakers' Society, the helpers seem to have been entirely

[30] Cf. "Industrial Remuneration Conference Report," pp. 114—118, paper on Skilled and Unskilled Labour in the Shipbuilding Trade, by J. Lynch.

[31] Cf. op. cit., pp. 117 and 118. This account is also based in part upon a personal interview with Mr. Lynch.

[32] Cf. "Newcastle Daily Leader," 1st, 2nd, 6th, and 8th February, 1886.

unrepresented. Had they possessed an organisation they could hardly have been placed in this melancholy position.

It is in this way, moreover, that increased organisation seems to have paved the way for increased harmony. A manufacturer of the north of England informed me[33] that, although he was not expressing the opinions of his class, yet he personally thought that employers had reason to be thankful to trades unions. He was not alluding, indeed, to the small unions, but to the large well-organised unions. For now, when disputes occurred, in small matters as in great, employers had not to deal with a large body of men of conflicting views, and to fear that, when they had arranged a settlement with some members of the body, they might find themselves still in conflict with others. But they now had the advantage of meeting a few representatives, and they knew that, if they could arrive at a settlement with them, their difficulties would be over for the time.

And there are collateral advantages attaching to this. In a large well-organised union it is probable that the best men will come to the front, and that they will bring the calmest heads and the widest experience—and withal a natural anxiety to relieve the strain occasioned by a dispute to the funds of the society—to bear on the negotiations into which they enter. It may be, indeed, and sometimes is, the case, that under the thoroughly democratic constitution which is characteristic of most trades unions—with the habitual reference of questions to the decision of the whole body—the advice of the officials may be overborne by an impulse of prejudice or passion. But the fact still remains that the opinions of the officials are, in the nature of things, likely to have considerable weight, and that the course of the negotiations will, in all probability, run more smoothly when the employers meet the same, or very nearly the same, representatives on each occasion. The employers on their part, even if they are not regularly combined together into an association, are generally, in comparison with the men, so few in number, that they can readily unite together in such an emergency as a strike.

It may then perhaps be the case that the "principle of degene-"ration," by which, according to Jevons,[34] associations of men are subject to a tendency to fall away from their original purpose, may, in the case of trades unions, assume this pacific form. It may be that, as they have undoubtedly contributed to the *education* of the workman, in the broadest sense of the word, by acquainting him with some of the conditions of business and teaching him the

[33] *Cf.* Report of Royal Commission on the Depression of Trade for a similar testimony from a shipbuilder on the Clyde.   *Q.* 12018.
[34] *Cf.* "The State in Relation to Labour," by W. S. Jevons, pp. 124—127.

responsibilities of official position; as they have developed their function as friendly societies (a function, be it remembered, which was originally in some sense forced upon them in order to escape the disabilities of the law), and developed it to such a degree that it now occupies the most prominent position in their expenditure, so that, in the years 1876-80,[33] 1,393.466*l.* was spent on benefit purposes by seven of the most representative unions, as compared with 158,361*l.* on strikes; so in the future they may be chiefly known as the confessed promoters of peace. Mr. Frederic Harrison,[36] speaking at the Trades Union Congress of 1883, has called attention to a significant passage in the report of the parliamentary committee for that year: "The measure of value of "a strong Union lies not so much in the conduct of successful "strikes, as it does in the number of disputes its moral strength "prevents."

[33] *Cf.* "Contemporary Review," September, 1883; "The Work of Trade "Unions," by G. Howell. On one day during the winter of 1885-86, the Northumberland Miners' Association distributed 3,561*l.* in relief to 8,398 miners in thirty collieries. *Cf.* "Newcastle Daily Chronicle," 8th March, 1886.

[36] *Cf.* "Contemporary Review," October, 1883. "The Progress of Labour," by F. Harrison. *Cf.* also "Trade Unions," by W. Trant, pp. 100—106, and Typographical Association's Rules IV, XVII, XVIII.

CHAPTER III.

The Second Stage: the Creation of Boards of Arbitration and Conciliation.

We may now pass on to the consideration of what we have distinguished as the second stage in the peaceful settlement of industrial disputes. The uncertainty and friction which must almost of necessity attach to such occasional and irregular negotiations as those we have described in connection with the shipbuilding industry of the north, are chiefly due to the fact that the two parties are not accustomed to meet one another round a common table, and that they therefore come to the negotiations with a natural suspicion of each other's attitude and arguments. But if there is a regular board of conciliation in existence in the trade, or even if there has grown up a traditional habit of referring disputes to arbitration, then a presumption is established in favour of mutual concession or peaceful argument in lieu of a resort to actual force. There is an organised machinery in existence, and there is a habit, which may become almost instinctive, of using this machinery. The two parties are accustomed to meet one another, and to endeavour to oppose argument to argument rather than force to force; and they can scarcely pursue this practice without learning to recognise the difficulties which either side may have to confront, and without entering, to some extent at least, into the position of their opponents.

A. The board of conciliation and arbitration in the manufactured iron trade of the north of England, which we propose to take as the typical instance of this second stage, has now been in existence for some seventeen or eighteen years. Mr. Crompton[37] has drawn very marked attention to its formation and working. He maintains that there is no portion of industrial history which is more interesting than the improvement effected in the relations of masters and men in the manufactured iron trade of the north of England. For here there have been most exceptional difficulties to overcome.

[37] Cf. "Industrial Conciliation," p. 49.

(i). In the first place the trade itself has been subject to considerable fluctuation. Sir Isaac Lowthian Bell,[38] in examination before the Royal Commission on the Depression of Trade, states that " the conditions of producing iron in this country have varied " so greatly and so frequently in the last 30 or 40 years that the " trade, like that of metals generally, stands in a somewhat excep- " tional condition." He shows, both in his oral evidence before the Commission, and in a written statement[39] printed as an appendix, how the production of iron has shifted from district to district. At one time, in the year 1806, "31 per cent." of the iron made in the United Kingdom, amounting in all to 258,000 tons, was made in South Wales; and in the "North-Eastern district"—including Northumberland, Durham, and the North Riding of Yorkshire— the production at that time was "nil." In 1884, with a total production of 7,811,720 tons, the proportion supplied by Wales had fallen to 11 per cent.; that furnished by Staffordshire had declined from 19 to 7 per cent.; but on the other hand the North-Eastern district contributed 32 per cent. of the total production, and Cumberland and Lancashire 20 per cent. He adds that " changes of a similar character have affected the position of almost " all the seats of the iron trade;" and he specially alludes to the Cleveland district as "a striking example of a rapid develop- " ment." He calls attention also to the "excessive irregularity in " the demand " for iron,—a circumstance which "certainly does " not apply, at all events to the same extent, to other branches of " industry." "Iron being wanted for almost every industry, is " the one of them upon whose head the misfortunes of all the " other industries ultimately fall. If the cotton trade is bad, the " cotton spinners require less machinery. If the mineral trade is " bad, the railways require a smaller amount of accommodation; " fewer rails are required and less rolling stock. And the same " observation applies with regard to ships."

He specially indicates[40] the way in which that substitution of steel for iron, which seems to be, perhaps, the chief inventive change of the times, has affected the manufactured iron trade and diminished the number of puddling furnaces. In 1860 there " were " in existence some 3,000 to 3,500 of these furnaces." In 1870 the number had doubled, and amounted to 6,699; but "in this year " the value of the Bessemer process began to be recognised." Despite of this, however, the iron manufacturers continued to extend " their powers of production," and in 1875 the number of puddling furnaces had increased to 7,575. Another decade passed,

[38] Cf. Report. Q. 1929.
[39] Cf. op. cit., Second Report, part i, App. A (1).
[40] Cf. Ibid. Q. 1957—71.

and in 1884 there were only 4,577 furnaces, and many of these were standing idle. He also supplies a table of the annual production of manufactured iron between the years 1872-84 by " certain firms " in the North of England, which, he says, constitute " about nine-tenths of the makers there ;" and this table illustrates very vividly the fluctuating character of the trade. Perhaps the most noticeable fact is the remarkable and sudden decline in the rail trade about the year 1877; and there can be no doubt that, had it not been for a rapid extension in the contemporaneous demand for plates and angles in the shipbuilding industry, the diminution in the production of manufactured iron would have been " very much more alarming " and prolonged than was actually the case. This decline, indeed, in the iron rail trade, a s we shall subsequently notice, was so unmistakable, that masters and men declare before the arbitrator on different occasions that the iron rail trade is practically dead; but Sir Isaac Lowthian Bell says that the same fate which befell iron rails now " threatens to " overtake iron plates and angles for shipbuilding."[41]

Mr. Spence Watson, again, who has sat as arbitrator on four occasions, and has given a succinct but exhaustive account of the history of the board in a paper read before the Barnsley Chamber of Commerce,[42] writes that since the formation of the board "it " has been tested in every way. Prices have gone up to their " highest point and down to their lowest. There have been " 'booms' and intense depressions. Demand has far exceeded " supply, and has died away." The shorthand writer's reports[43] of proceedings at the different arbitrations supply abundant confirmation of this, and in the employers' rejoinder,[44] before Sir

[41] *Cf.* Report. *Q.* 10953, 11906.
[42] *Cf.* Lecture on Boards of Arbitration and Conciliation and Sliding Scales, by R. Spence Watson. Extracted from the " Barnsley Chronicle " of 20th March, 1886.
[43] As frequent reference will have to be made to these reports, it will abbreviate the notes to distinguish and refer to them by numbers as below :—

I.	Arbitration before Mr. Dale in July, 1877.	
II.	,,	Shaw-Lefevre in December, 1878.
III.	,,	Dale in August and October, 1879.
IV.	,,	J. W. Pease in April, 1882.
V.	,,	Sir J. W. Pease in November, 1882.
VI.	,,	Mr. Spence Watson in January, 1884.
VII.	,,	,, April, 1884.
VIII.	,,	,, November, 1884.
IX.	,,	,, October, 1885.

All these reports are printed and published at the Ironworkers' Association Office, Grange Road, Darlington, and I have to thank the secretary of the association, Mr. Edward Trow, for kindly supplying me with copies.
[44] *Cf.* V, p. 7.

Joseph Pease, in November, 1882, we find the significant assertion that "anticipations in connection with the iron trade are always " doubtful, and the foresight of the most experienced is of little " real use." The following table, which illustrates the greater part of the history of wages and of arbitration in the trade, proves that this language is by no means exaggerated, and we may fairly say that the board of conciliation in the manufactured iron trade of the north of England has had as serious difficulties to confront in the way of changes in the conditions of industry as could well be imagined :—

TABLE I.

Number of Settlement.	Date of Settlement.	Occasion and Nature of the Wages Settlement.	Duration of Settlement.	Average Selling Price of Iron.[1]	Amount over Shillings for Pounds [2]	Wages Arranged [3] (Long Weight)	Percentage of Advance or Reduction.
				£ s. d.	s. d.	s. d.	Per cent.
—	1869 [4].........	—	Jan.—April inclusive	—	1 9	8 -	—
1	May, 1869...	Mr. R. Kettle's award	May—Dec. inclusive	6 11 3[5]	2 6[6]	8 6	+ 56
2	Jan., 1870 ...	Mr. T. Hughes' award	1870	7 - 11 25[7]		9 6	+ 10
3	Feb. 6, 1871	Mr. T. Hughes' award [9]	Jan. 1—June 30, 1871	7 - 8[8]	varying to	9 -	- 5
4	July 25, 1871	Mr. T. Hughes' award (in London). Workmen claim advance	From July 1, 1871 ...	7 2 0·25[10]		9 6	+ 5
5	Oct. 17, 1871	Employers give 5 per cent. advance on condition of acceptance of sliding scale	Until March 31, 1872	—[12]	1 9	10 -	+ 5
6	Oct., 1871 ...	Sliding scale arranged by Mr. D. Dale [13]	For 3 months ending June 30, 1872	7 16 6·15[14]	2 9	10 6	+ 5
7	July 22, 1872	The figures for the three months ending May 31, 1872, gave an advance of 7½ per cent.; but a few days after an advance of 20 per cent. was given to the men in Staffordshire, and this created dissatisfaction in the North of England. At a meeting of the Board the employers gave an advance, in addition to the 7½ per cent., of 12½ per cent., thus equalising the rates with those in Staffordshire [15]	To March 31, 1873 ...	8 11 6·82	4 -	12 6	+ 20
8	April, 1873	Mr. R. Kettle's award at Saltburn [16]	To Sept. 30, 1873......	10 12 10	2 6	13 3	+ 7½
9	Oct., 1873 ...	Mr. R. Kettle's award at Durham. Employers claim reduction of 12½ per cent.	Till end of 1873	11 19 3 63[17]	—	13 3	=[18]
10	Dec. 19, 1873	Conference of employers and men from north of England and Staffordshire at Birmingham, and mutual reduction of 7½ per cent.[19]	Jan. 3—April 4, 1874	11 15 8·42	—	12 6	- 7½
11	April 10, 1874	Meeting of the same at York, and reduction of 10 per cent. agreed upon, after which Derby sliding scale to come into operation [20]	April 4—July 4, 1874	11 18 3 38	—	11 6	- 10

TABLE I—Contd.

Number of Settlement.	Date of Settlement.	Occasion and Nature of the Wages Settlement.	Duration of Settlement.	Average Selling Price of Iron.			Amount over shillings for Pounds.		Wages Arranged (Long Weight).		Percentage of Advance or Reduction.
				£	s.	d.	s.	d.	s.	d.	Per cent.
12	1874 21	Derby sliding scale	For 3 months ending								
			Sept. 30, 1874	10	18	11·78²²	-	9	11	9	+ 2½
			Dec. 31, 1874	9	19	1·08	-	9	10	9	-10
			March 31, 1875 ...	9	1	5·13	-	9	9	9	-10
			June 30, 1875	8	14	3·09	-	9	9	6	- 2½
13	July 15, 1875	Mutual arrangement at Darlington between employers and men of north of England 23	Till end of 1875	8	3	1·23	-	9	9	-	- 5
14	Jan. 18, 1876	Messrs. Williams and Mundella's award 24	Jan. 17—Aug. 17,1874	7	10	4·09	-	9	8	3	- 7½
15	Aug. 2, 1877	Mr. Dale's award at Darlington. Employers claim 10 per cent. reduction	Till Dec. 31, 1877 25...	6	17	1·43	1	6²⁶	8	3	=
16	April 13,1878	Mr. Dale's award 27	—	6	7	4·01	1	3	7	6	- 7½
17	Jan. 13, 1879	Mr. Shaw-Lefevre's award at Darlington. Employers claim reduction of 5 per cent.28	For 2 months, and thenceforth subject to 1 month's notice	6	-	5·37	1	-	7	-	- 5
	Sept.18,1879	Mr. Dale's award in the matter of a special claim for reduction of 15 per cent. in the wages of shinglers, rollers, heaters, and shearmen 29	—	—			—		—		-12½
18	Sept. 18,1879	Mr. Dale's award at Darlington. Employers claim reduction of 5 per cent.30	Till December 21, and then subject to 1 month's notice	5	7	7·41	1	6	7	-	=
19	Dec. 22, 1879	Employers concede advance of 12½ per cent.32a	Till May 1, 1880	5	5	-32b	3	-	8	3	+12½
20	Dec. 22, 1879	Sliding scale fixed by award of Mr. Dale (April 23, 1880) on basis of 1s. 6d. over shillings for pounds.31 Sliding scale was to last for two years, May 1, 1880—May 1, 1882	For 3 months ending								
			July 31, 1880	6	2	11·45³²	1	6	7	9	- 5
			Oct. 31, 1880	6	10	8·95	1	6	8	-	+ 2½
			Jan. 31, 1881	6	8	0·01	1	6	8	-	=
			April 30, 1881	6	4	3·96	1	6	7	9	- 2½
			July 31, 1881	6	3	7·45	1	6	7	9	=
			Oct. 31, 1881	6	2	1·74	1	6	7	6	- 2½
			Jan. 31, 1882	5	19	8·04	1	6	7	6	=
			April 30, 1882	5	18	11·16	1	6	7	6	=
21	Feb. 6, 1882	At meeting of Board by mutual arrangement. Advance of 7½ per cent. conceded 33	Till April 29, 1882 ...	5	18	11·18	2	3³⁴	8	3	+ 7½
22	April 29,1882	Mr. J. W. Pease's award at Middlesbrough.35 Workmen claim advance of 7½ per cent. for current quarter, and arbitrator is empowered to settle wages from May 1 to October 28, 1882. He awarded:—	Till Oct. 28, 1882......	6	2	11·23		—32c		—	
		May 1—July 31, 1882. No alteration	May 1—July 31, 1882	—			—		8	3	=
		August 1—September 16. 2½ per cent. advance	Aug.1—Sept.16,1882	6	6	11·97	—		8	6	+ 2½
		September 16—October 28. 2½ per cent. advance	Sept. 16—Oct. 28,1882	—			—		8	9	+ 2½
23	Nov. 23,1882	Sir J. W. Pease's award at Middlesbrough. Workmen claim advance of 7½ per cent., and employers a reduction of 7½ per cent.	Till last Saturday in February, 1883, and then subject to 1 month's notice	6	8	6·49	1	9³⁶	8	3	- 5

TABLE I—*Contd.*

Number of Settlement.	Date of Settlement	Occasion and Nature of the Wages Settlement.	Duration of Settlement.	Average Selling Price of Iron.	Amount over Shillings for Pounds.	Wages Arranged (Long Weight.	Percentage of Advance or Reduction.
				£ s. d	s. d.	s. d.	Per cent.
24	Mar. 19, 1883	Durham agreement between master and men, by which existing rates of wages were continued until September 29, and then a sliding scale was to come into force similar to the former one	Till Sept. 29, 1883 ...	6 6 -	2 -	8 3	=
25	Mar. 19, 1883	Sliding scale as above [37]	For 2 months ending[36] Nov. 30, 1883 ...... Jan. 31, 1883	6 2 4·08[39] 6 - 6 66	1 6 1 6	7 6 7 6	− 7½ =
26	Jan. 24, 1884	Mr. R. S. Watson's award at Newcastle. Employers claim reduction of 5 per cent.	For 3 months ending March 29, 1884	5 17 11·34	1 6[41]	7 6[40]	=
27	April 18, 1884	Mr. R. S. Watson's award at Newcastle. Employers claim reduction of 10 per cent.	April 12—June 28, 1884	5 13 7·20	1 6[41]	7 3	− 2½
28	June 9, 1884	Mutual arrangement between employers and men.[42] Employers claim reduction of 10 per cent.	For 3 months to September 27, 1884	5 8 11·41	1 6[45]	7 -	− 2½
29	Dec. 1, 1884	Mr. R. S. Watson's award at Newcastle. Employers claim reduction of 5 per cent., and workmen claim advance of 5 per cent.	Sept. 27—last Saturday in Jan., 1885	5 1 8·57[43]	—	7 -[46]	=
30	Oct. 28, 1885	Mr. R. S. Watson's award at Newcastle.[44] Employers claim reduction of 7½ per cent.	For 3 months	17 7·75[47]	1 9	6 9	− 2½

NOTES *to preceding* TABLE.

1 The average selling price is based upon the prices of bars, angles, plates, and rails. *Cf.* II, 9.

2 The custom of the trade is to pay shillings of wages (and a certain amount over) for pounds of prices. *Cf.* II, 9.

3 There are two weights: imperial ton = 2,240 lbs., and long weight = 2,400 lbs., and the custom in the trade was to pay by long weight; and even when in 1879 they were compelled by Act of Parliament to pay imperial weight (cf. II, 1), still the calculations continued to be based upon long weight. (*Cf.* VI, 4.

4 This was the year in which the Board was formed. The figures from this time to January 18, 1876 (inclusive), are based partly upon the figures supplied to Mr. Dale as arbitrator in July, 1877, and extracted from the minutes of the Board. *Cf.* I, 18.

5 The average selling price for the previous yearly period, and based upon the statements of orders upon the books, and the prices to be realised from them. These returns were not subjected to verification by an accountant until February, 1872. *Cf.* I, 11, 15.

6 5 per cent. advance in other tonnage rates = 6d. per ton on puddling. *Cf.* II, 10; VI, 3.

7 *Cf.* I, 15.

8 Prices on books, but the award, according to the men (*cf.* II, 7), was really based on the prices quoted in the "Iron and Coal Trades Review," which averaged 6l. 12s. 6d.

9 Against this award the men protested. *Cf.* III, 20.

10 *Cf.* II, 7.

11 *Cf.* statement in Mr. J. W. Pease's award. IV, 24.

12 The principle was now adopted of fixing the rate of wages in accordance with the returns of selling prices in the past. *Cf.* II, 7.

13 The wages for the ensuing quarter were to be based upon the selling prices of the preceding quarter.

14 The returns of Mr. Waterhouse, the accountant to the Board, here begin. These are the figures for the three months ending February 28, 1872, and are obtained by examination of the employers' books according to a method fully described below. *Cf.* VI, 7, and *infra*, p. 67.

15 *Cf.* IV, 7.

16 On this award the men base a contention that as wages have not followed prices in this case up to their highest point, so they ought not to follow them down to their lowest point. *Cf.* IV, 7.

17 The prices were also placed before the arbitrator of the returns up to September 30, and = 11l. 12s. 5·99d. *Cf.* IV, 7.

18 = signifies that no alteration was made by the arbitrator. *Cf.* IV, 7.

19 A basis for a sliding scale for the two districts was also agreed upon, and a joint committee appointed to arrange details. *Cf.* IV, 7.

20 Meetings of the joint committee were held at Derby and London. At York the North of England employers at first demanded a reduction of 20 per cent., but the Midland employers suggested a compromise of 10 per cent. *Cf.* IV, 8.

(ii). But the history of the successful working of the board is instructive on several other accounts, and it is hard to suppose that any board of conciliation could have greater difficulties with which to contend than those which have been triumphantly overcome in the case of the manufactured iron trade of the north. And hence we may fairly argue from its undoubted success to the likelihood of equal, and if possible greater, success in other industries and other districts.

Previously to the formation of the board the relations between masters and men seem to have been of the most unfriendly description. The trade itself had been characterised by a development of

---

[21] The figures from this point to December 31, 1881 (February 6, 1882), are based partly on those placed before the arbitrator by the employers on January 4, 1884 (cf. VI, 3 and 4), and, so far as mere accuracy goes, recognised as correct by the men. Cf. VI, 4.

[22] Based upon the prices for the three months ending May 31. Obtained in a manner described below. Cf. I, 11.

[23] At a meeting at Newcastle on March 6, 1875, the North of England employers resolved to give notice of the discontinuance of the scale after the 30th of June following. I, 18. The masters say this was necessitated by the decline of the iron rail trade. I, 11.

[24] At this arbitration a single umpire, together with two arbitrators, was appointed, and the award was made by the arbitrators. The award gave great dissatisfaction to the men, and they claimed that a new principle was introduced, i.e., that the decision was based on the depression of trade, and not on the selling prices. Cf. I, 6; 1, 17; VI, 11.

[25] And thenceforward subject to three months' notice of alteration.

[26] It seems to have been about this figure, and to have risen to 1s. 9d. and 2s. Cf. VI, 5.

[27] The men contend that this award was not based upon selling prices. II, 6.

[28] The men contend that the words of the arbitrator show that the award was based not upon selling prices, but upon Staffordshire rates. Cf. VI, 5. Here too there was a single umpire together with two arbitrators. VI, 11.

[29] Some doubt was felt as to the exact interpretation of the award, and Mr. Dale was asked his opinion upon the matter in October. At this meeting the nominal 12½ per cent. on the gross earnings, and the 8⅓ per cent. on the net earnings, was modified to 7½ per cent. (cf. III, 21). But the "helpers" still objected, and Mr. Dale sat as arbitrator in a case where the helpers at Consett were specially concerned, on November 29, 1879, and a further modification seems to have been made (cf. IV, 19). An unsuccessful appeal was also made to Mr. Dale on November 27, 1880, and to Mr. J. W. Pease on April 15, 1882, to restore this special reduction. Cf. IV, 19 (= 22 in the table.)

[30] This award established no "permanent" relation between selling prices and wages (cf. III, 15).

[31] In the previous negotiations the employers offered shillings for pounds, and the men claimed 1s. 6d. The employers then advanced to 1s. 3d., and the decision between this and 1s. 6d. as the basis of the scale was referred to Mr. Dale, who fixed it at 1s. 6d. Cf. VI, 4 and 5.

[32] These figures are for the quarter ending March 31, 1880, &c., and so on throughout the scale. Cf. VI, 3.

[32a] Cf. IV, 9. Given in consideration of the American boom, and in anticipation, and to induce the acceptance of the sliding scale, but not "justified" by actual results. IV, 11, 24; VI, 10, 14; VII, 9.

[32b] Cf. VI, 13.

[32c] The amount of shillings for pounds would apparently be for No. 1 in the table 2s.; 2, 2s. 6d ; 3, 2s ; 4, 2s. 6d.; 9, 1s 3l ; 10, 9d ; 11, 6d. below shillings; 22, 2s. above shillings, 2s. 3d., 2s. 6d.; and for No. 29, 2s. The general principle on which the calculation is made is seemingly of the following nature: for every pound, one shilling; for every quarter of a pound (i.e., 5s.), a quarter of a shilling (i.e., 3d.). Until prices have reached the half-crown, coming half way between the 5s., wages are calculated on the basis of the previous 5s., but when prices have passed beyond the half-crown, on the succeeding 5s. Thus on the basis of 1s. 6d. over shillings for pounds, 5l. would give 6s. 6d ; 5l. 5s., 6s. 9d.; 5l. 10s., 7s.; 5l. 15s. 6d., 6s. 6d.; 5l. 3s. 6d., 6s. 9d. Cf. IX, 5. Cf. also "Sliding Scales in the Iron Industry," by J. E. C. Munro, p 10.

[33] The men were dissatisfied with the amount of prices for the quarter ending December 31, 1881, and some of them intimated by notice to the employers their intention of stopping work after January 31, 1882. The Board passed a resolution stating that immediate inquiry should be made into the question of wages, but that all must continue at work. In some cases, however, a stoppage actually took place, and a demand for 7½ per cent. advance was conceded by the Board on February 6.

[34] Cf. Mr. J. W Pease's award. Cf. IV, 23.

[35] Cf. 29 supra. A strike followed this award, but Mr. (then Sir) J. W. Pease was again selected as arbitrator in November. Cf. V, 6. The award was partly based on prospective prices.

[36] Cf. VI, 6.

[37] Notice was given on November 23, 1883, to suspend the scale on December 29, 1883.

[38] Prices were to be ascertained every two instead of every three months. Cf. VII, 6.

[39] = prices for the two months ending August 31, 1883.

[40] Cf. VI 6; VII, 9.   [41] Cf. VII, 4.   [42] Cf. VIII, 3.

[43] The application of the award dated from October 1, and the last ascertainment previous was for July—August, and = 5l. 3s. 11 cnpd., but the arbitrator had also before him the September—October returns. Cf. IX, 10.

[44] The question of a sliding scale had been discussed since the last arbitration. IX, 4.

[45] Cf. IX, 4.   [46] Cf. IX, 6 and 17.   [47] Cf. IX, 10.

N.B.—For the compilation of this table I ought to say that I am solely responsible. Errors of detail may have crept in, and the table is unfortunately not complete in all particulars. But I have endeavoured to secure as much completeness and freedom from error as the examination of the reports of arbitration cases has enabled me to attain, and in a number of instances I have fortunately had the opportunity of copying verbatim from these reports. The particular sources of my information on each point are indicated in the preceding notes.

extraordinary rapidity. The labour, Mr. Crompton[45] tells us, had been chiefly supplied by immigrants from other districts or trades, and among their number were several Irishmen. The sudden increase in the population of Middlesbrough between 1861 and 1871[46] abundantly illustrates this point, and the men employed in the trade were thus to a large extent complete strangers to the masters. This fact alone was of very unfavourable promise for the existence of amicable relations.

The labour again of puddling iron calls for a considerable amount of hard physical toil, and is so exhaustive in character that it is anything but calculated to promote intellectual self-culture among the workmen in their leisure hours.

In this respect at least there can be no doubt that the substitution of steel for iron is attended by great advantage. For, by the Bessemer process of manufacturing steel almost direct from the blast-furnace, and the Gilchrist-Thomas and other modifications of that process, the exhaustion of the iron puddling-furnace[47] is avoided, and the burden of the physical labour is shifted from the shoulders of men on to the shoulders of nature. The change has indeed its melancholy side, for, like most similar changes, it is apparently producing a temporary displacement of specially-trained labour. But if there is any truth in Mr. Nasmyth's assertion, that " if you call for the brute force of a man, you will degrade the " man," and will compel him to seek excitement rather than intellectual improvement in his leisure hours,[48] then on this ground, if on no other, the change is to be welcomed.

Again and again at courts of arbitration do the workmen's representatives allude to the exhaustive nature of their work. Thus in July, 1877, we read in the workmen's reply :[49] " In no trade are " workmen subject to more physical exhaustion than in the iron " trade .... in fact the nature of our employment is so dirty, " disagreeable, and uncertain that very few can be induced to enter " it, and from its exhaustive nature men are unable to follow their " employment after reaching 45 or 50 years of age .... A few " years at the puddling furnace makes a man prematurely old, " saps his energy, and makes him unfit for further employment." Before Mr. Shaw-Lefevre in December, 1878, the workmen maintain a similar position.[50] " We would," they urge, " ask them " (i.e., the employers) " to pause and consider the laborious nature

---

[45] Cf. " Industrial Conciliation," p. 51.   [46] 108 per cent.

[47] It should be noticed, however, that machinery has also been invented to relieve the labour of the puddling furnace.

[48] Cf. Tenth Report of Trades Union Commissioners, 1868, p. 65, quoted in the " Economics of Industry," I, VIII, 9.

[49] Cf. I, p. 8.   [50] Cf. II, p. 4.

" of our work, the vast numbers that have left our trade, never
" to return, the difficulty in inducing youths to enter a trade so
" exhaustive, uncertain, and unremunerative in its character." And
again,[51] " It is well known that our labour is the most exhaustive
" and disagreeable that is voluntarily undertaken by man, and as
" Mr. C. M. Palmer, M.P., stated, unfit for human beings to per-
" form; that in no trade do workmen destroy so many clothes
" and shoes, require so much food to support and enable them to
" follow their employment; that no trade is so uncertain," and in
no other trade do " men suffer so much loss of time on account of
" sickness caused by physical exhaustion, inability to continue at
" work during hot weather, breakages, and various other causes
" over which men have no control." Nor are these statements
put forward by one side only, for Mr. Whitwell, an employer and
President of the Board, affirms[52] before Mr. Dale, in August, 1879,
that "ironworkers' labour is hard."

We may, then, readily believe that a puddler, who was asked to
speak at a meeting at Sunderland, was expressing a great deal of
truth in a small number of words, when he said that he was sorry
that he had been asked to speak, because he was " *not educated, but*
" *was a puddler*," and the comment of one of the workmen's delegates at the board upon this is very significant, and can hardly be
suspected of excessive exaggeration. " Puddlers," he says, " as a
" class are not very intelligent, and if they were very intelligent
" they would not be puddlers."[53] We need not therefore be
astonished, the wonder would rather be that it should be otherwise,
if we meet with evidence to which we may again have occasion to
refer—of difficulty experienced in some instances by the representatives of the men in obtaining the adherence of their constituents to
the decisions of the board. Thus the workmen state before the arbitrator in April, 1882,[54] that " at various times the existence of the
" board has been jeopardised, but the loyalty of the majority has
" enabled us to be successful." And again,[55] " many times owing
" to the action of either employers or workmen, the continuance of
" the board has been in great danger." Mr. Trow, the workmen's
secretary,[56] urges before the arbitrator at Newcastle, in January,
1884, that he is " often told " that he is an " employer's man," and
the employers frankly recognise the difficulties of the position
occupied by the representatives of the men. Thus Mr. Whitwell,
in July, 1877, says,[57] that he quite admits that there is " an amount

---

[51] *Cf.* II, p. 17.   [52] *Cf.* III, p. 11.
[53] *Cf.* IX, p. 18.   *Cf. contra*, VI, p. 12.
[54] *Cf.* IV, p. 6.   [55] *Cf.* IV, p. 16.
[56] *Cf.* VI, p. 19.   [57] *Cf.* I, p. 17.

" of covert irritation[58] throughout the lodges connected" with the
board, and he adds, " we have no opportunity to know exactly
" how strong it is, and therefore I feel great sympathy, more than
" I would like to express at this table, for the operative members
" present at this meeting. They have a great deal to contend with.
" Whereas we only represent our individual firms, they speak for
" hundreds and thousands of men, who all have something to say
" to them when they meet them at their various meetings."
The arbitrator himself, who was on that occasion Mr. Dale, says[59]
that he believes the difficulties of the workmen have been great
in inducing large bodies of men to appreciate the reasons for
their conduct at the meetings of the board.

But if there are these difficulties connected with the working of
the board, the position of affairs previous to its formation was still
more unpromising. In 1866 there was a strike and lock-out lasting
for some five months, and " producing a great deal of misery on the
" one side, and a great deal of poverty on the other."[60] This was
followed by an arrangement among the masters for " combined
" action," and the formation of a large " guarantee fund," out of
which payment was to be made to employers who were " troubled
" by strikes," as compensation for any reasonable loss they might
thus have sustained. The relations between the two parties, which
indeed were far from amicable before this, now became even more
unfriendly, and we find more than one allusion[61] in the arbitration
reports to this unsatisfactory state of affairs. In 1869, however,
steps were taken which led to the formation of a board of conciliation
and arbitration. A demand for an advance in wages had been made
by the men, and their representatives met the masters at a conference, and it was as the outcome of this conference that the board
was established. The plan on which it is formed is described in
detail by Mr. Watson in the pamphlet to which we have referred,[62]
and in its broad outlines it may be said, if we except the absence
of a legal character and of legal sanctions, to resemble the constitution of the French and Belgian *conseils de prud'hommes*,[63] and
may be taken as a type of most, if not all, of the boards of conciliation and courts of arbitration established in this country.

(B). It is of the following nature. The men belonging to the
different works are represented in each case by one delegate who is
chosen by ballot, and the employers, after a similar fashion, have
also in the case of each firm a single representative. The members

[58] This feeling seems to have been occasioned during a special dispute with a particular firm.

[59] *Cf.* I, p. 18.

[60] *Cf.* II, p. 9.   [61] *Cf.* I, p. 6; VI, p. 18.

[62] *Cf.* " Boards of Arbitration," &c., pp. 3 and 4.

[63] *Cf. infra*, p. 29.

of the Board elect a President and one Secretary from among the representatives of the masters, and a Vice-President and a second Secretary from among the representatives of the men. There are also two auditors, two treasurers, and a referee. Besides this a Standing Committee is elected by the Board, consisting of five representatives (exclusive of the Vice-President) of the men, and ten representatives (exclusive of the President) nominated by the employers, five of whom alone are able to discuss or vote upon any question; for the larger number is merely allowed to meet the difficulty occasioned by the greater frequency with which the employers, as contrasted with the men, may be called away from home upon business-engagements. The President and Vice-President, who are by virtue of their office members of all committees, have no power of voting. The regular meetings of the Board are held twice a year, and on other occasions when specially summoned by the Standing Committee, which holds its own meetings every month, or, should business require, at more frequent intervals.

All questions are in the first instance investigated by the Committee. They must be submitted in writing to the secretaries seven days before the meeting, and the written reply of the other side is usually laid before the same meeting. " Prior to the investigation " an agreement of submission is signed " by the representatives of the employers and employed concerned in the matter under dispute. Should the Standing Committee be unable to agree, the assistance of the referee, who has power to take evidence, is invoked. All questions can be settled in this way with the exception of a general rise or fall in wages and the appointment of an arbitrator; and these can be determined by the Board alone. The Board also decides matters referred to it from the Standing Committee, and selects an arbitrator if it cannot itself arrive at an agreement.

The arbitrator holds a " court," as it is called, at a time and place which he appoints. Some time before the court sits, the party making the application furnishes the arbitrator and the individual members of the board with a printed statement of the arguments on which it bases its claim, and the opposing party replies with a printed answer. " The members of the Board attend " the court;" the advocates appointed by either side commence the arguments for and against the application; the discussion is continued, and opportunity given to any member of the board, who is desirous of so doing, to contribute his share. The arbitrator requires any evidence which he considers necessary; and, when he has determined upon his award, it is printed and sent to each member of the board. The necessary expenses connected with the board are defrayed by the subtraction of 1d. every fortnight from the wages of every workman who earns from 2s. 6d. a day, and by the payment by each firm of an amount equal to that deducted from the wages of the workmen in their employment. All members of the board, employers and employed alike, are paid at one and the same rate out of these common funds.

(c). With some exceptions, then, on points of detail, to which we shall afterwards allude, the broad outlines of this system reappear in the constitution of most of the boards of conciliation and courts of arbitration established in this country; and there can be little doubt that the type on which they have been modelled is the constitution of the " conseils de prud'hommes " found on the Continent in France and Belgium. The features of these "conseils " de prud'hommes " have been familiarised to English economic students by the description given of them in Jevons's " State in " Relation to Labour."[64] He traces their origin to the " experts " or " prud'hommes " selected by the mediæval French guilds to appraise the genuineness of manufactured goods, and to adjust such disputes as might arise between manufacturers and merchants at the various markets and fairs. He shows how such institutions of this character as still survived were abolished at the revolution ; how scarcely a decade passed before the necessity of some form of trade-tribunal was felt by the city of Lyons at least, and how the " conseil " which was legally established there became the type of similar tribunals in other towns.

The members of these French " conseils " are, he states, elected in equal numbers respectively by masters and men, the " maire " performing the functions discharged by our English overseers in connection with the registers of parliamentary electors, and the " préfet " taking the part of our returning-officer. The president, however, and vice-president are nominated by the central government. The "conseil " retains its authority for three years, and is divided into two bureaux or committees. The " bureau particulier," consisting of one master and one man, sits every day for two hours ; and the disputants are, in the first instance, "invited " to come before this bureau to explain their difficulties and to arrive, if possible, at an amicable settlement by means of conciliation. Should this result, however, not be attained, they are then *formally summoned* before the "bureau général," which must be composed of five members at least, and holds weekly meetings. The " bureau général," after the same fashion as an English arbitrator, disposes authoritatively of the matter.

(i). Here then we have a legalised machinery of arbitration and conciliation. The " conseils " seem upon the whole to have worked with considerable success. Mr. W. H. S. Aubrey, in an eulogistic

---

[64] *Cf.* " The State in Relation to Labour," pp. 159 and 160.

article in the "Contemporary Review,"[65] shows by an "illustrative
"instance" how "substantial justice" may be obtained through
their agency in a brief space of time and at a nominal cost; and
M. Chevalier is said to have termed them "une des plus nobles
"créations dont notre siècle s'honore."[66]

But from an English point of view there seem to be considerable
disadvantages inherent in their constitution; and these disadvantages attach to them by reason of their legal character. The "maire"
of the "commune," as we have noticed above, is to prepare the voting
lists; the "préfet" is to act as returning-officer; the president[67] and
vice-president are—or were until lately—to be nominated by the
executive government; and petitions for the establishment of the
"conseils" are to be addressed to the Minister of Commerce. The
"conseils" are thus closely connected with the municipalities; and
Mr. Aubrey draws attention to an incidental drawback attaching
to this when he states that in Paris, with all its variety of trades,
there are only four separate "conseils." The appeal again from
the decisions of the "bureaux" lies to the "tribunals of com-
"merce," and failing these, to the civil courts.[68] It is true that
Mr. Aubrey tells us that few such appeals are made, but the fact
that this provision exists is corroborative proof,—if proof be
needed,—of the legal character of the "conseils;" and he also
states that in districts where there are no "conseils" established,
the matters which would come under their cognisance are decided
by the ordinary "justices of the peace."

(ii.) Now, the first and fundamental objection to this legal
character is that it is not in harmony with English traditions or
inclinations. It has been forcibly argued by Mr. Rae[69] in his
"Contemporary Socialism," that the "secret of the pathetic story
"of modern France" is to be found in its "over-government."
Revolution has followed revolution; but, with every change in the
form of government, its authority has remained the same. "The
"struggle for freedom has thus been corrupted into a struggle for
"power." This tendency has thoroughly permeated the theory
and practice of the French; and a familiar but instructive indica-

[65] Cf. "Contemporary Review," April, 1883, vol. xliv, "Conseils de
"Prud'hommes," by W. H. S. Aubrey.

[66] Cf. Report on the Practical Operation of Arbitration and Conciliation in
the Settlement of Differences between Employers and Employees in England, by
J. D. Weeks, p. 2, sec. I.

[67] M. Leroy-Beaulieu alludes to a "loi nouvelle qui donne aux conseils de
"prud'hommes le droit de choisir eux-mêmes leur président" (cf. "Essai sur la
"répartition des richesses," 2nd edit., 1883, p. 394); but I have not been able to
discover the particulars of this law.

[68] E.g., the Court of Cassation.

[69] Cf. "Contemporary Socialism," by John Rae, pp. 23 and 24.

tion of this is to be found in the ambition commonly attributed to the ordinary French boy of becoming a government official.[70]

But in England there can hardly be said to be as yet any such decided tendency. There was scarcely anything more significant than the difference of attitude exhibited[71] by French and English working-men, at a conference of trades unionists held in 1883 in the French metropolis, and attended by a deputation from the English trades unions. The former looked to the State as the one agency of economic improvement; the latter, taught by the history of the past, felt and maintained that they must rely in the main—as they had done with conspicuous success—upon their own efforts for their own amelioration. A similar difference of attitude was shown at the Industrial Remuneration Conference which met in London in the January of 1885, and may be seen by comparing a paper read[72] by a representative of French workmen, a M. Adolphe Smith—a delegate, it is true, of the " Fédération des " Travailleurs *Socialistes* de France," but still a writer whose paper contains sufficiently typical indications of the general position of French workmen—with the papers[73] of Mr. J. G. Hutchinson and —more especially—of Mr. J. Mawdsley. And in considering this point—as indeed in considering the general question of conciliation—it must be borne in mind that the operation of any system of industrial arbitration or conciliation must command the active support, or at least insure the acquiescence, of trades unionists, if it is to succeed in the primary aim it ought to have in view—the aim of minimising the friction between employers and employed.

It is true indeed—and should be mentioned—that upon this special point there is some evidence of a contrary effect to that to which we have already alluded. For the President of the Trades Union Congress at Southport in the autumn of 1885 declared that it was his opinion[74] that the time had " arrived for compulsory " arbitration ;" and the legal sanction of the principle which does exist on the English statute-book was apparently due in a great degree to the efforts of trades unionists.[75]

But it can hardly be doubted that the balance of evidence shows that there is likely to be far more opportunity for the growth of

[70] *Cf.* " The Man *versus* the State," by Herbert Spencer, pp. 30 and 31.

[71] *Cf.* " Trade Unions," by W. Traut, p. 63. This report was written before the meeting in Paris in 1886, but the text would be in the main correct even if it were applied to this later meeting. *Cf.* also Second Report of the Royal Commission on the Depression of Trade, part II, App. E, p. 135.

[72] *Cf.* Industrial Remuneration Conference Report, p. 473, &c. The *italics* are my own.

[73] *Cf. op. cit.*, especially pp. 57, 58, and 160.

[74] *Cf.* Report of the Eighteenth Annual Trades Union Congress, held at Southport, 7th—12th September, 1885, p. 18.

[75] *Cf.* " Conflicts of Capital and Labour," by G. Howell, X, 32 ; XI, 4.

amicable relations where compulsory action is absent. Mr. Weeks,
in an exhaustive report on arbitration and conciliation furnished
to the Government of the United States of America in 1878,[76] states
that the " conseils de prud'hommes " themselves have not proved
as successful in Belgium as they have been in France, and the
reason he urges for this result is that the Belgian conseils " have
" in some cases criminal jurisdiction." And, were there no other
evidence of English opinion forthcoming, it would be sufficient to
point to the fact that there is provision upon the English statute-
book for legalised arbitration, and that this provision apparently
remains a dead letter.

Jevons alludes[77] to a " series of acts " passed in the eighteenth
century " for the settlement of disputes in particular trades ;" and
states that these various acts were " consolidated " in an act of the
fifth year of the reign of George the Fourth,[78] which apparently
still remains in force, and established a " general law relating to "
the " arbitration of disputes in every branch of trade and manu-
" facture." The arbitration was to be effected by the agency of a
body of " persons "—consisting of equal numbers of masters and
men—" nominated by the justice of the peace." Out of this body
the disputants were on either side to choose one referee, and the
referees thus selected had full powers to decide the matter. In
case, however, of disagreement, other referees " could be appointed,
" and, in the last resort, the justices " of the peace might settle
the dispute.

So late, again, as the year 1867,[79] an act was passed to establish
" councils of conciliation " in England, after the model of the
French " conseils." The Queen or the Home Secretary could grant
a license for the formation of such a council, on the presentation of
a joint petition from any number of masters and men who had
resided for six months previously in the district, and—in the case of
the men—had worked for seven years previously at the trade. The
council, which was to be elected by the petitioners in the first
instance—and afterwards annually by all inhabitant householders
who enjoyed similar qualifications—was to consist of not less than
two or more than ten masters, and two or more than ten men—
three of whom were to constitute a quorum—together with a
chairman who was to have a casting vote, and was not to be
connected with the trade. A committee of conciliation " appointed
" by the council, and consisting of one master and one workman,"
was to try to reconcile the disputants in the first instance; and

Cf. Report of J. D. Weeks, p. 2, sec. I.
Cf. " State in Relation to Labour," p. 151, &c.
5 Geo. IV, cap. 96.
Cf. op. cit., pp. 161—163 ; 30 and 31 Vict., cap. 105.

then, should the attempt fail, the matter was to go before the council. Its award was to be final, and might be enforced by " distress, sale, or imprisonment."

An Arbitration Act[60] was also passed in 1872, at the instance of Mr. Mundella. This Act gave facilities for the creation of an elastic system of arbitration, the local details of which were to be laid down in each case in an agreement made between individual master and individual workmen, and were therefore to be binding as part of the contract of hiring.

Here then we have the machinery for legalised arbitration, and yet it seems never to have been put into working. Mr. Bevan, indeed, in the paper upon strikes to which we have before referred,[61] recommends the establishment of a system in England analogous to that of the French " conseils "—with twelve councils in different districts of the kingdom, and a superior board of appeal. But this seems, if we may say so, to be rather the opinion of an outsider than the opinion of those acquainted with the internal relations of industrial workers.

The reports of the Royal Commission on the Depression of Trade supply some meagre information upon the point, but the evidence thus obtained is conflicting. Among the answers furnished by different Chambers of Commerce to the questions addressed to them by the Commissioners, we find that the Metal Trades' section in London is " very much in favour " " of the establishment of " boards of arbitration and conciliation between masters and " workmen, to minimise the national loss from strikes :" and would apparently wish such boards to be established by legislation.[2] The Macclesfield Chamber of Commerce thinks that a " remedy " for " unfortunate misunderstandings between capital and labour," " might be found in the establishment of boards of arbitration and " conciliation, similar to those in existence on the Continent."[3] But the North Shields and Tynemouth Chamber, while advocating " a board of arbitration between capital and labour," and holding that " the want of sympathy between capital and labour has tended " to strangle trade," thinks that such a board " would be beneficial " independently of legislation."[4] The Derby and Hull Chambers allude to " strikes and the fear of strikes," but do not advocate any method of conciliation.[5] In the evidence given before the commissioners, we find Mr. Holmshaw,[6] a representative of the Sheffield

[60] 35 and 36 Vict., cap. 46.
[61] Cf. supra, p. 5.
[2] Cf. Second Report, part I, App. B, p. 393, ans. 13 (a).
[3] Cf. First Report, App. A, p. 96, ans. 14 (a).
[4] Cf. op. cit., p. 107, ans. 13 and 14 (a).
[5] Cf. Second Report, part I, App. B, pp. 386—387, ans. 10 and 14.
[6] Cf. Q. 1215—47.

D

Trades Council, stating that if a "council or chamber of industry,"
consisting of an equal number of representatives of operatives and
of manufacturers or middlemen, "were invested with power to
"settle by *amicable*[87] negotiation the rate of wages by piecework"
in certain of the Sheffield trades it "would be a powerful agency
"for preventing strikes," and for "bringing about a better under-
"standing between capital and labour," and would be warmly
welcomed by the trade-societies. And Mr. Albert Simpson,[88] a
cotton-spinner at Preston, is of opinion that "*tribunals* of arbitra-
"tion" "would not answer."

An opinion has indeed been put forward that the existence of
such a legalised machinery for the settlement of industrial disputes
as official tribunals of arbitration, would tend to diminish the
frequency, and to mitigate the severity, of these disputes, even if
recourse to it were optional and not compulsory. But there does
not seem to be any more adequate reason for incurring the expense
necessitated by the establishment of such a machinery, than there
was for passing an Agricultural Holdings Act in 1875, out of the
provisions of which the parties concerned could at once contract
themselves, and then arguing that it had proved useful as a pattern
on which to model voluntary agreements between landlord and
tenant with regard to compensation for unexhausted improvements.

(iii.) If indeed the two parties of employers and employed
looked with favour upon the institution of legalised industrial
tribunals, it is doubtful whether there are not further disadvantages incidental to such a method of procedure, and whether these
disadvantages are not of so grave a character as to outweigh any
possible advantages. For we are at once confronted by the
imminent probability of the growth of a body of elaborate law
attaching to the practice and decisions of these courts. In France
indeed, according to Mr. Aubrey, no argument is admitted at the
time of hearing but merely a simple statement of the case and
equally simple explanations. In England the act of 1867 laid
down the important principle that "no counsel, solicitors, or
"attorneys" were to be heard before the councils or committees
without the consent of both parties. But against this we have to
set the fact that a body of law has actually grown up around the
French conseils, and that more than one special manual upon the
subject has proceeded from the pen of French advocates. And
the danger of the growth of elaborate technicalities, and possibly
of a regular body of professional advocates, is forcibly illustrated
by the experience of voluntary arbitration, and the tendency
there exhibited to institute and enforce precedents. Thus in the

---

[87] The *italics* are my own.   [88] *Cf.* Q. 5193.

Northumberland coal trade, we find the men protesting[59] before the arbitrator in December, 1875, against the action of the employers[90] in carrying back their comparison of wages and prices to 1871, and thus apparently "ignoring" the award of Sir Rupert Kettle in March, 1875, instead of using that as a basis for the case now before them; and Lord Herschell himself in his award expresses[91] his agreement with the view urged by the men "that the last "award ought, as a rule, to be taken as the starting point." "To "act otherwise," he adds, "would be to necessitate going over the "same ground on every occasion that a difference arises as "to wages, and to prevent anything like a settled system being "arrived at. Prior matters ought only to be looked to, I think, "on clear proof of misapprehension or mistake." Despite of this, in the next arbitration before Sir Lyon Playfair in September, 1876, we find the same complaint urged by[92] the men about the action of the masters, and a similar expression of opinion from the mouth of the arbitrator. Nor are the facts dissimilar from this in the case of arbitrations in the manufactured iron trade of the North of England. Objection is also raised, as we shall sub-sequently notice, both in the Northumberland coal trade and in the manufactured iron trade, to changes in the general character of the basis on which the award is to be given—whether for instance the relation of wages to selling prices is to be the guiding con-sideration, or whether the current wages in other districts, and such circumstances as depression in trade, fluctuations in the labour market, and alterations in the cost of materials and of management, are to be taken into account.

Changes, too, in the method of procedure are jealously watched In the iron trade Mr. Cullen objects[93] before Mr. Dale in 1877—an objection indeed which is overruled by the arbitrator—to an "innovation" by which the employers' case is to be read and opened by a master other than the employers' secretary. "It is "different," he urges, "to what we have done before, and we "should not allow any changes to crop up at these arbitrations "without explanation." And later on he contends:—"It is our

---

[89] Cf. II, pp. 22 and 25. We shall have occasion to refer more than once to three cases of arbitration in the Northumberland coal trade; and it will abbreviate the notes if we distinguish the reports (copies of which I owe to the kindness of Mr. Ralph Young, Secretary of the Northumberland Miners' Mutual Confident Association) as under:—

K, report of arbitration before Sir (then Mr.) R. Kettle in March, 1875.

H,   "   Lord (then Mr.) F. Herschell in December, 1875.

P,   "   Sir (then Dr.) Lyon Playfair in September, 1876.

[90] Cf. II, p. 7.   [91] Cf. II, p. 237.
[92] Cf. P, pp. 28 and 132.   [93] Cf. I, p. 4.

" duty to prevent any innovations on the recognised forms of the
" Arbitration Board, because, if we once break the rules, we may
" never see the end of it." And his colleague, Mr. Trow, adds:—
" In every case that crops up there is something new introduced
" by the employers' side. We first fixed on a basis to settle wages,
" and that was abandoned by the employers. Now we have a
" precedent established the first time that this Board" "met, and
" acted upon on every occasion since, about to be departed from
" because the present secretary is not so well able to take the case
" as Mr. Jenkins."[94]

But if there is, almost of necessity, this tendency to create and
appeal to precedents, and a consequent liability to dispute which
of two conflicting precedents should be adopted in the particular
case under discussion, it seems to be in the highest degree
probable that, if once a legal character were given to the system,
these precedents might be multiplied on precedents until it might
require experts to deal with them, and that that desire to get at
the truth—if necessary—by an informal method which is evinced[95]
by different arbitrators might be effectually crippled by obligatory
compliance with rigid forms. Industrial disputes might, indeed,
be settled by this method; but the irritation which prompts to
the dispute would remain, and the peace thus obtained would be
hollow and insecure.

(iv.) But there is an objection still more fatal than those we
have already mentioned to the interference of the law in these
matters. In the English acts of 1824 and 1867, there is an express
declaration that the authoritative settlement of industrial relations
for the future is not to be intrusted to the legalised courts or
committees. Thus in the first of these two acts the provision is
inserted[96] that "nothing in this act contained shall authorise any
" justice or justices acting as hereinafter mentioned, to establish
" a rate of wages, or price of labour or workmanship, at which the
" workman shall in future be paid, unless with the mutual consent
" of both master and workman." And the act of 1867 in a similar
way declares[97] that "nothing in this act contained shall authorise
" the said council to establish a rate of wages or price of labour
" or workmanship at which the workman shall in future be paid."
Mr. Mundella's Act of 1872 would indeed permit this settlement
of wages for the future, if such a provision were inserted in the
agreement between masters and men; but, as such an agreement
is part of the contract for hiring, and only in force so long as the

[94] Cf. for similar cases of insistance upon precedent IV, p. 4; IX, p. 3.
[95] Cf. 1, p. 5; K, pp. 28, 34.
[96] Cf. 5 Geo. IV, cap. 96.
[97] Cf. 30 and 31 Vict., cap. 105.

relation between employer and employed continues, the legal compulsion would have little practical effect, and therefore in this respect the act may be likened to the act of 1824.[98] Mr. Weeks, it is to be remarked, states[99] that the continental conseils are similarly destitute of powers to settle wages for the future, except by mutual agreement.

But these are the very questions on which it is most important to obtain a settlement if the course of industry is to run smoothly; and it might possibly be argued, in answer to the considerations we have advanced above, that it is because the laws have contained no provision for the compulsory arrangement of these questions, that they have proved a dead letter. On the other hand it is clear that, were they to meet this requirement, they would as a matter of fact be reverting to a condition of affairs not very dissimilar from that which prevailed when the justices of the peace settled the wages of the district; and this can hardly be seriously desired.

D (i). It is I think also apparent that conciliation is far more satisfactory in industrial matters than arbitration, and that indeed mutual concession is as much to be preferred to authoritative arbitration, even when the reference to arbitration is voluntarily made, as willing arbitration is to be preferred to the compulsion of a legalised tribunal. Even under the French system of legalised arbitration, out of thirty or forty thousand or more cases annually submitted to the *conseils*, some 70 per cent. appear to be settled by the conciliatory action of the " bureau particulier." [100] In the manufactured iron trade of the north of England during the seventeen years of the existence of the board of conciliation and arbitration, the Standing Committee had, up to the 1st of March, 1886, held 276 meetings, and adjusted nearly 800 disputes, while the board itself had only met 97 times, and in some 17 cases alone had reference been made to arbitration.[101] At the annual meeting of the board held on 1st February, 1886—at which it is worthy of notice that the president expressed[102] a hope that " before long there would be " an organisation in connection with the shipbuilding trades some- " thing like that which existed amongst the iron trade, by which " reference to an arbitrator could be made "—the report for the year stated that " with one exception, the committee had been able

[98] *Cf.* " Industrial Conciliation," pp. 143, 172.

[99] *Cf.* Report, p. 2, sec. I.

[100] *Cf.* Statistical Society's *Journal*, vol. xliii, pp. 35—64, Mr. Bevan's paper on " Strikes of the Past Ten Years," March, 1880.

In Belgium the proportion settled by conciliation appears to be somewhat similar.

[101] *Cf.* " Boards of Arbitration," &c., pp. 4 and 5, and Table I, *supra*, p. 21.

[102] *Cf.* " Newcastle Daily Leader," 2nd February, 1886. There is an apparently permanent referee, who is consulted by the Standing Committee, and an arbitrator may be appointed for special occasions by the board. *Cf. supra*, p. 28.

" to dispose of all the cases brought before them without the
" necessity of calling in the referee."

In the Durham and Northumberland coal trades, where, as we
shall see hereafter, sliding scales have been in successful working
for some years, the general principle of conciliation and arbitration has been applied during a still longer period, but latterly
since the introduction of the sliding scale it is conciliation which
has been chiefly employed. In the Durham trade a joint committee of masters and men was formed some fourteen years
ago, and is now composed, according to Mr. Watson,[103] of twelve
members—six selected by the Durham Coalowners' Association,
and six by the Durham Miners' Association—and a chairman
chosen annually by the two associations. All disputes arising
at particular collieries between masters and men which are
laid before the committee, may be settled by its own decision or
referred to arbitration ; and, should the arbitrators disagree about
the appointment of an umpire, the selection is to be made by the
Judge of the Durham County Court. A considerable number of
cases come before the committee ; for even under a sliding scale
there are occasions for minor disputes, as wages still vary from
colliery to colliery, or even from seam to seam, according to the
special degree of difficulty of working. In most of these cases, which
numbered 390 in the year 1881, and in 1882 amounted to 493,
in 1883 to 562, and in 1884 to 629, arbitration is not invoked; and
in 1883 only 37 of the 562 cases were referred .to arbitration, and 17
were reported upon by persons "nominated to inquire into the facts."
In 1884 23 questions were treated in this latter fashion, and 45 were
settled by arbitration. In Northumberland[104] also a joint committee was founded upon a similar basis in March, 1873, to discuss
" all questions " (according to a statement made[105] at an arbitration
in March, 1875) " of mere local importance affecting individual
" pits or portions thereof." Six members of this committee are
chosen, as in Durham, by the masters' association (the " Steam
" Collieries' Defence Association "), and six by the miners' union
(the "Northumberland Miners' Mutual Confident Association"). At
first, unlike the Durham board, its decision " was not to be final,
" but was to take the form of a recommendation," and to be submitted for approval or rejection to the votes of the general body
of the trade. But since then the rules have been remodelled, and
now, as in Durham, its decision is final. During its existence it has
adjusted with very little delay more than 3,000 questions.[106]

---

[103] Cf. " Boards of Arbitration," &c., pp. 6 and 7.
[104] Cf. op. cit., p. 10.   [105] Cf. K, p. 6.
[106] Mr. Watson says "not more than half a dozen days have been lost
" throughout its entire jurisdiction." Cf. p. 10.

Joint committees have similarly been formed in other coal mining districts,[107] as for instance in Cumberland in connection with the sliding scale arrangement of 1882, where the committee consists of four coalowners and four representatives of the men, and a secretary appointed by either side; and in South Wales a joint committee was established in 1875, and consisted originally of five representatives of either side, but the number of this committee has since undergone some modification. The principle of conciliation has also been successfully introduced into other trades, and notably by Mr Mundella into his own trade of hosiery at Nottingham in 1860. Here, where the board consisted, according to Mr. Weeks,[108] of twenty-one members annually elected, there was a triple provision for conciliation. Endeavours to arrange disputes were to be made in the first instance by the two secretaries. Then the matter was to be brought before a committee of inquiry, consisting of two representatives of either side; and only in the third place, if reconciliation were not previously effected, the board was to decide the question. Should there be disagreement here, provision was made for the intervention of a referee.

(ii). The advantages of conciliation over arbitration, as the evidence we have mentioned abundantly indicates, are in a certain sense obvious, but they will perhaps be brought into clearer relief by the negative method of examining the difficulties and disadvantages attaching to arbitration. It must, however, be premised that it seems to be necessary to make some provision for resort to arbitration. There must be a final court of appeal, though that court be habitually kept in the background; for otherwise there will be no way out of a deadlock. Nor must it be forgotten that in cases where there is no permanent board of conciliation in existence it is sometimes found better to end a dispute by reference to a neutral arbitrator.

For an illustrative instance of the necessity of this provision for the occasional intervention of an arbitrator, we may take the lace trade at Nottingham. Mr. Brooksbank, the president of the Lace Manufacturers' Association, and also of the board of conciliation, states, in his evidence[109] before the Royal Commission on the Depression of Trade, that there are three branches in the Nottingham lace trade : the lace used for millinery, dress, and

---

[107] *Cf.* "Sliding Scales in the Coal Industry," by J. E. Crawford Munro, pp. 32, 34 and 35, 37 and 39.

[108] *Cf.* "Report on the Practical Working of Arbitration and Conciliation in "the Settlement of Differences between Employers and Employés in England." By J. D. Weeks, sec. iii, p. 6.

[109] *Cf.* Report, Q. 6602. Originally there seems to have been a standing referee. *Cf.* "Industrial Conciliation," p. 46. This board has now ceased to exist.

fancy purposes, the lace used for curtains, and the lace used for
plain nets; and that there are three corresponding sections of the
board of conciliation. Each section meets and arranges the prices
to be paid for various kinds of work, and if the members of the
section fail to come to an agreement the matter is brought before
the whole board. "But," he adds, "one weak point in our
" present arrangement is, that if we fail to agree we must either
" lock the men out or the men strike; in fact the men refuse to
" allow any question to be referred to any referee."

A way out of a deadlock of this nature may be provided in
more than one direction, but in the final resort there must
inevitably be a single arbitrator, referee, or umpire. In the
manufactured iron trade of the north, if the standing committee
fail to come to an agreement, the referee, whose appointment is
apparently permanent, is summoned; and in a similar way, if the
board cannot agree upon any point, an arbitrator is chosen. In
the Durham coal trade questions are sometimes referred by the
joint committee to an umpire, and sometimes to persons nominated
to inquire into the facts, and before the construction of the
sliding scale in March, 1877, disputes about the general rate of
wages had for some time been adjusted by arbitration. In the
Northumberland coal trade a similar practice has been followed,
and like provisions appear to exist in connection with most of the
sliding scales[110] which have been put into operation.

If indeed the chairman of the committee or board be invested
with a casting vote he has, for all practical purposes, the power of
an arbitrator; and in the case of the sliding scale arranged in the
year 1877 in the Durham coal trade,[111] the chairman of the joint
committee is actually named as umpire in the event of any
dispute arising, and, should he be unable to act himself, he is
to appoint some other umpire in his stead. In the manufactured
iron trade of the South Staffordshire district, wages have been
arranged by the president of the board since the abolition of the
sliding scale in September, 1883;[112] but in this case, on the
reconstitution of the board, which was effected some years ago,
a provision was made[113] for the election of a president who could
take no part in the discussion, but enjoyed the possession of a
casting vote. In this way the delay caused by the necessity
of specially summoning the referee, on particular occasions when

110 Cf. "Sliding Scales in the Iron Industry." By J. E. Crawford Munro,
pp. 29, 35, 38, and 41. Cf. also "Sliding Scales in the Coal Industry," pp. 21,
31, 45, 50, and 53.

111 Cf. op. cit., p. 21.

112 Cf. "Sliding Scales in the Iron Industry," p. 17.

113 Cf. "Industrial Conciliation," p. 64.

his intervention was required, was avoided; and in addition to the president the board has also a chairman.[114] There seems indeed to be considerable weight in the argument urged by Mr. Mundella,[115] that it is more in accordance with the principle of conciliation, and more likely to conduce to the permanence of amicable relations, if there is discussion at the meetings of the boards and the committees without actual voting. Each party should endeavour to work towards a common unanimous agreement, and then, should this prove impossible, a referee should be summoned who should indeed be a member of the board, but should attend those meetings alone where his presence is needed to adjust a dispute, or, at least, should only intervene where his mediation is required. Mr. Whitwell, the president of the board of conciliation in the manufactured iron trade of the north, who has frequently acted as the employers' advocate at courts of arbitration, states himself[116] before Mr. Watson in April, 1884, that he is "placed in an awkward position in being president of " the board and advocate for the employers as well," and that he " would rather occupy the judicial position of president." And from this we may fairly argue *à fortiori* that a chairman or president of a board who has, unlike Mr. Whitwell, the possession of a casting vote, is better situated if he has no direct interest in the matters he is called upon to decide, and is not an active contributor to the discussions which take place, or the arguments which are advanced.

(iii) (a). Some provision, then, it is clear, for a final appeal to a single individual is necessary. But it seems equally evident that the occasions for such an appeal should be reduced to as limited a number as possible. For there are, as we stated before, several difficulties attaching to arbitration. There is one indeed which is involved, in only a less degree, in conciliation, and that is the possibility that the decision may not be loyally accepted. That this may happen, even in the case of conciliation, is proved by the occurrence of strikes against the decisions of the joint committee in the Durham coal trade. But Mr. Watson states[117] that since the formation of the committee the strikes, which have indeed been only of a local character, have been also " of short duration," and that a "very small percentage" alone have been against the decisions of the committee. " The stoppages of work," he adds,

---

[114] *Cf.* VIII, p. 14.

[115] *Cf.* " Economics of Industry," by A. and M. P. Marshall, III, VIII, 1. *Cf.* also " Industrial Conciliation," p. 36. In the Nottingham Hosiery Board the chairman had at one time a casting vote, but Mr. Mundella says that this casting vote was always getting them into " trouble."

[116] *Cf.* VII, p. 12.

[117] *Cf.* " Boards of Arbitration," &c., p. 7.

" from whatever cause, have steadily decreased, and were in 1884 " scarcely one half of what they were in 1882." And, with regard to the Northumberland committee, he affirms[118] that " its decisions " have scarcely ever been called in question, and no serious opposi- " tion to them has been raised upon any occasion." In the case of conciliation indeed it is very unlikely that adherence should not be given to the decision of the committee or board. For, when once the principle has become thoroughly established, the two parties meet prepared to arrive at a mutual agreement, and are ready to give and accept concessions, to discuss arguments with fairness, and weigh them with carefulness and without bias; and they do not come to the meetings of the board or committee with the intention of enforcing at all hazards a foregone conclusion. The spirit in which the decision is obtained is likely to be the spirit in which it will be observed.

But in the case of arbitration there is *ex hypothesi* initial disagreement between the two parties, and either side in the nature of things cannot help feeling that its case is the stronger It is indeed for this reason that the argument sometimes advanced for the legalisation of courts of arbitration has some weight, for the decision of the arbitrator would thus be accompanied by a legal sanction. Under Lord St. Leonards' Act of 1867[119] it might be enforced by proceedings of distress, sale, or imprisonment; and in the Wolverhampton building trades, where a permanent arbitration court for the three trades of plasterers, carpenters, and bricklayers was established by Sir Rupert Kettle,[120] and lasted until the year 1875, when the bricklayers and plasterers seceded in consequence of dissatisfaction felt by the former with reference to a particular award, a code of working rules was drawn up by the representatives of the employers and the employed, and posted in the different workshops. A breach of this code was a breach of contract, and could be legally punished. In the pottery trade, where, Mr. Weeks[121] tells us, there had been no general strike between 1836 and the time when he was writing (*i.e.*, 1878), a clause had been inserted in the contracts for hiring, providing for the reference of disputes to arbitration; and Mr. Mundella's Act of 1872[122] seems to have aimed at an object somewhat similar to this. But there appear to be very powerful reasons for excluding law and lawyers as such from the matter, if there is to be any genuine feeling of conciliation as the result of acts of conciliation. There may however be an agreement of a definite character,

[118] *Cf. op. cit.*, p. 10.
[119] 30 and 31 Vict., cap. 105. *Cf. supra*, p. 32.
[120] *Cf.* " Strikes and Arbitrations," by R. Kettle, p. 35, &c.
[121] *Cf.* Report, p. 3.   [122] 35 and 36 Vict., c. 46.

binding in honour, whatever may be the case at law, between the
two parties to an arbitration. In the manufactured iron trade
of the north an agreement of submission has to be signed by the
representatives of the employers and the workmen concerned in
a dispute, before the standing committee commences its investigation of the affair. And even if such an agreement is not put
into writing, it is generally taken for granted, and in the majority
of cases the decisions of industrial arbitrators are loyally observed.
There are however instances to the contrary effect.

In the manufactured iron trade of the north we find more than
one allusion[123] to dissatisfaction felt on the part of the men at the
influence of the board of conciliation upon their position as
compared with that of the workmen in other districts and trades.
A formal protest seems to have been raised against the award of
Mr. Hughes in February, 1871, and a successful appeal was made
to Mr. Dale in 1879 to explain, if not to reconsider, a decision he
had given in an arbitration affecting the wages of special classes
of ironworkers.[124] An actual strike, though of a momentary nature,
appears to have taken place against the first award of Sir
Joseph Pease in 1882,[125] and indeed immediately previous to that
award there had been a suspension of work on the part of some of
the operatives, in violation it is true of a special resolution of the
board, which had not apparently been fully understood, but also it
appears in contravention of the habitual and recognised rules.[126]
The employers on their part are charged by the operative delegates
with infringement of the principles[127] and actual rules of the board,
both in meeting[128]—with the best intentions, it is admitted, but
still in direct violation of principle—the men who had ignored the
authority of the board on this occasion, and pledging themselves,
through the mouth of the president, to vote for an advance in
wages if the men would on their side resume work; and in
enforcing at other times alterations in the conditions of working
without allowing the men affected the right of appeal to the board.
And Sir Joseph Pease in his award states[129] his opinion that the
operatives alleged, as he thought, " with considerable truth, the
" fact that their loyalty to arbitration had stood the test better
" than had always been the case with some of the employers."
But he adds that he " recognised on both sides a strong desire to
" do that which was right and reasonable, and abide by the
" decision of an arbitrator in whose award one side or the other

[123] Cf. I, pp. 5 and 16; II. p. 16; IV, p. 6; V, p. 3.
[124] Cf. III, pp. 17—21; IV, p. 19, &c., and IV, p. 5.
[125] Cf. V, p. 6.   [126] Cf. IV, p. 7.
[127] Cf. VIII, p. 5.   [128] Cf. IV, pp. 7 and 8.
[129] Cf. IV, p. 24.

" might not fully unite, rather than jeopardise the enormous
" industries in which they were mutually so greatly interested."

And against the facts which we have mentioned above we have
to set no little amount of evidence of an opposite character. " The
" partial stoppage of works," urges[130] Mr. Trow, the advocate for
the men in 1877, " on one or two occasions owing to misunder-
" standing, has in the north of England been within the narrowest
" possible limits . . . . . and the career of our board has been one
" of almost uninterrupted triumph and success." And seven years
later, after the board had had to pass through troublous waves,
we find him asserting before Mr. Watson in November, 1884, that
" during the fifteen years preceding " the previous " December the
" board " had "been the most successful institution in settling
" wages, locally or generally, of any institution that was ever
" established in connection with the trade of this or any other
" country." " I challenge," he eloquently adds, " the employers or
" any historian to point to a parallel in the history of the trade of
" the whole universe, where so many disputes have been settled
" amicably, where such a strong confidence has been established
" between employers and employed, or where such a spirit of
" conciliation has been displayed between employers and workmen,
" as has been displayed in this district during the fifteen years of
" this board's existence."[131]   Nor is this in any sense the language
of empty exaggeration; for on the 4th of October, 1881, Mr. Dale
was publicly presented with his portrait at Darlington as a
testimony to his services in connection with arbitration, and at
the gathering of representatives of capital and labour which took
place upon that occasion, abundant testimony was borne to the
" undeniable success of arbitration in connection with[132] the north
" of England iron trade;" and the loyalty evinced both by
employers and employed to the principle met with ample recognition.

(b). The second disadvantage attaching to arbitration is closely
connected with the first, and it is this: there is necessarily an
element of contentiousness in arbitration proceedings. The two
parties come before the arbitrator resolved to secure victory if possible, and to prove that the position of the other side is untenable,
and that its arguments are inconclusive. But in the case of
conciliation they are—or should be—desirous of arriving at a
common agreement by means of mutual concession. It is true
that the discussion before an arbitrator may be conducted with
perfect courtesy, and indeed with few, if any, exceptions it is
so conducted. In the Northumberland coal trade for instance

[130] Cf. I, p. 5.
[131] Cf. VIII, p. 4.   Cf. also II, p. 4.   [132] Cf. IV, p. 6.

we find the two parties commencing their cases with appreciative remarks of their opponents. The owners speak[133] of the miners as forming, "both physically and morally, a most advanced type of " mankind, from which some of our most talented and clever " inventors and senators have been drawn, and from which, with " great skill and judgment, some of the ablest advocates have been " selected that ever represented any body of men." They allude[134] more than once to the friendly relations which have existed in the trade, to the absence of any great strikes, and to the adjustment of difficulties by amicable negotiation and conference; and they express a hope that these relations may continue. The miners, on their side, refer[135] in similar terms to the "tone and spirit" in which the employers' case is advanced before Sir Rupert Kettle, in March, 1875. They accept "frankly, in the spirit in which it is given," the offer of the employers to submit certain accounts to the inspection of the "umpire," and they do not attempt to throw any doubt upon " the mathematical accuracy of the figures given, or to call in ques- " tion the fairness of the data supplied " to the accountants who have prepared the statement in question. On both sides again there is evidence of a desire to be fair and accurate in their arguments. The owners[136] "have endeavoured to conduct" their "investigations " with perfect fairness and justice to both parties." They "are " willing and wishful and desirous to lay everything fair and " above-board open to " the umpire.[137] The men acknowledge[138] the difficulty the owners may feel in acquainting them with the details of their accounts, and hold that it would be "unjust and " ungenerous not to admit that large sums have been expended by a " majority of the employers in building new houses of a better kind, " and in improving the old houses " provided for their miners[139] and not to take this into account in discussing the monetary value and pecuniary expense of such accommodation. The arbitrators, again, on successive occasions, take the opportunity afforded when giving their awards to recognise the fairness and justice of either side. Sir Rupert Kettle alludes to " the implicit confidence with which " each side has received any verbal statement from the other " during the whole progress" of the arbitration, and to "the thoroughly friendly spirit in which, from first to last, the discus- " sions have been conducted."[140] Lord Herschell affirms that the arbitration "could not possibly have been conducted in a more " excellent spirit or more ably than it was."[141] And Sir Lyon Playfair

---

[133] *Cf.* K, p. 2 ; P, pp. 23, 24, and 82.
[134] *Cf.* K, p. 2 ; H, p. 6.   [135] *Cf.* K, pp. 42, 56, and 114.
[136] *Cf.* K, p. 13.   [137] *Cf.* H, p. 8.
[138] *Cf.* H, p. 10.   [139] *Cf.* P, p. 19.
[140] *Cf.* K, p. 129.   [141] *Cf.* H, p. 240.

expresses[142] his "strong sense of the eminent fairness and ability" with which the arbitration "has been conducted on both sides."

Similar language is to be found in the awards and utterances of arbitrators[143] in the manufactured iron trade of the north. Warmth is indeed displayed by the different parties in urging their views ; but Mr. Shaw-Lefevre in 1878, in answer to a remark from one of the employers, apologising for the unusual noisiness characterising their proceedings, says[144] that he has "nothing to " complain of ;" and Sir Joseph Pease in 1882 thinks[145] that he " may congratulate both sides on the way " the "matter has been " discussed. There have been," he states, "strong remarks, but " not an irritative word." Mr. Watson in April, 1884, uses very significant language to a similar effect : " I can only say," he remarks,[146] " that to me sitting here and hearing the arguments " which have been adduced, and remembering what it all means, " and the personal importance of the issues to those who have " been debating the questions—I must say that I have felt more " impressed than ever with the vast advantage and importance of " a Board of Arbitration and Conciliation like this. It has been " my fate in life to attend many hot discussions where the matters " in debate have not been of that immediate advantage to persons " discussing them ; but the fact that it is possible to discuss such " questions with so much calmness and fairness is a very gratifying " one indeed."

The employers here, as in the Northumberland coal trade, recognise the courtesy of the operatives. The President acknow- ledges[147] in 1877 the "good feeling" with which the case has been argued "on both sides ;" and on the same occasion another employer expresses a " hope that the operatives will understand " that the employers " have no desire to hide anything from them," and have tried to be as "frank" as their opponents, and as " temperate and " moderate " as they can. "If any remark has fallen from me," he adds, "that could not be supported and sustained by facts," " I hope" "that it will be overlooked." "We have attempted," says[148] the President, again, addressing the arbitrator in 1882, " to " put before you, Sir, the case for the employers honestly and I " hope fairly, and I am sure from the men's side it has been fairly " done." And, before Mr. Watson in 1884, he says[149] that if he has " hurt" the feelings of the men, he is "exceedingly sorry," and that the employers are willing to "withdraw" any remarks which

---

142 Cf. P, p. 134.
143 Cf. II, p. 16 ; IV, pp. 22—24 ; VII, p. 13 ; VIII, p. 17, and IX, p. 22.
144 Cf. II, p. 16.   145 Cf. IV, p. 22.
146 Cf. VII, p. 13.   147 Cf. I, p. 25.
148 Cf. IV, p. 23.   149 Cf. VII, p. 12.

have had such an effect. And later in the year he declares[150] that
he wishes to see "fairness" dealt to "both sides," and that he
"himself will always try to see that facts and figures before" them
"shall be viewed from both sides." More than once, again, the
employers express[151] their sympathy with the operatives, both with
the representatives themselves and with their constituents; and on
one occasion[152] the period of holding the arbitration was postponed
for two months, in order to secure the presence of the workmen's
secretary, who had been ill at the time.

The men on their side do not fail to make known[153] before
Mr. Shaw-Lefevre in 1878 their sense of the courtesy of the
employers. Their secretary says on this occasion, "We have
" always treated each other with courtesy, and have accepted the
" statements of each other. We do sometimes say hard things
" of each other when we get heated, but as soon as the meeting is
" over we forget them." And on another occasion he remarks,[154]
" We cannot but admire the conciliatory spirit in which we have
" been met to-day, and we will try to reply in the same spirit. You
" know that, as a rule, there is no ill-feeling around this board;
" although we may get warm sometimes, it is simply the result of
" excitement that we get into, and our earnestness in defending the
" cause we advocate."

The President of the Board himself describes[155] in 1878 the
history and character of the Board, in words which may be
employed as a summary of the evidence we have just been considering. "We have had," he says, "considerable experience of
" the working of arbitration, and it has been our custom to tell
" each other the truth as far as possible round this table . . . .
" Since the formation of the Board we have had very few
" difficulties or differences amongst its members. We have varied
" in our opinions, and I think we may truly say we have learnt to
" respect each other. I think that statements made from either
" side of the table are believed by the other side. There was a
" time when each side was inclined to doubt each other. We have
" gained wisdom by experience, and learnt to respect the views of
" each other, and learnt to believe in the statements made by each
" side."

But, despite of this evidence, it is hardly to be supposed that
when either party has pecuniary interests at stake, and on one side
at least it may well be that the very means of subsistence are
imperilled; when either party is endeavouring, with all the force
and abundance of argument that it can command, to convince the

---

150 Cf. VIII, p. 15.
151 Cf. I, pp. 9 and 12; II, p. 14.
152 Cf. VIII, pp. 3 and 9.
153 Cf. II, p. 15.
154 Cf. III, p. 13.
155 Cf. II, p. 9.

arbitrator of the justice of its own contention and the erroneous
nature of that of its opponent; and when they both know, as
Sir Joseph Pease remarked[156] on one occasion, that somebody must
be " hurt " by the award on whichever side it may be—under such
a condition of things as this it can hardly be supposed that arbitration is not calculated to excite some contentiousness, and in all
probability to leave behind a little soreness of feeling. Either
party may, as Sir Joseph Pease adds, learn the difficulties which its
opponents have to confront, if it hears those difficulties stated in
the strongest terms and enforced with the greatest emphasis at an
arbitration court, but in the nature of things it can hardly help
feeling that its own difficulties are sterner and more serious. The
regular statement then of arguments on either side seems not
unlikely to accentuate the grounds of mutual opposition, and the
irregular discussion of points which may arise incidentally during
the arbitration is calculated to create some feeling of irritation.

(c). This consideration naturally conducts to another objection.
In an arbitration case either side is eager to bring forward any and
every argument which is likely to tell for its advantage, and hence
the discussion must be carried to a considerable length. This evil
may, to some extent, be avoided by the observance of a definite
form of procedure, and by the selection of an arbitrator who is
thoroughly conversant with the details of the trade. The first of
these provisions is generally, if not universally, adopted; and
indeed some irritation is felt and some objection raised if any
departure is made from the established procedure.

The details of the procedure may indeed be varied from time
to time, and the court may sit for a longer or a shorter period.
But in its broad characteristics it remains unaltered, and in some
instances there has been, as we have before noticed, an insistance
on rigid and almost pedantic adherence to recognised forms which
seems to emphasise the danger, if a legal character were given to
these courts, of sacrificing the spirit of conciliation to the letter
of legal technicality, and of calling into being a body of professional advocates, whose services would be absolutely needed to
understand and handle the precedents which might, in industrial
as in other matters, be multiplied on precedents according to
the traditional usage of English law. Defined, however, as the
procedure is in its main outlines, it is open to variation on
points of detail; and even in its broad characteristics it admits
of lengthy and almost prolix discussion. And indeed, if the real
facts of the case are to be brought within the cognisance of the
arbitrator or umpire, there must be an elasticity of detail and a

possibility of prolonged investigation. Thus Sir Rupert Kettle, sitting as arbitrator in the Northumberland coal trade, insists[157] that the parties to the case have not come there to "reserve or hold "back anything," and he disclaims for himself any intention to give countenance to the theory sometimes propounded that arbitrators' awards are given by "some splitting of the difference," or "softening the way," or "making things pleasant." On his part he requires "to go to the root of the matter minutely as a "man of business before" he gives his "judgment." In a similar spirit Lord Herschell is reported to have said that[158] he would not "confine" the discussion "in any technical way," but, if any fresh point was dealt with at any stage which the other side had not "heard before, he should always desire that the matter should be "discussed until each side had heard all that the other has to put "forward." And in the iron trade, Mr. Dale really sums up the "matter by saying,[159] We want to get all the facts out. We don't "want to stand on a mere formality."

(1). If indeed the arbitrator is thoroughly conversant with the details of the trade, there is less necessity for elaboration of argument or prolonged discussion. This familiarity with detail may be secured by the appointment of an arbitrator who is himself a member of the trade. To this course, however, it is obvious that there may be objections; for it may conceivably arouse suspicions of bias in the minds of either side, and, though these suspicions may be entirely unfounded, yet they are hardly unnatural.

For, as Mr. Dale points out in 1877,[160] the feelings not merely of the representatives of either party, who may be proof against any tendency to mistrust the arbitrator—who, indeed, in the majority of cases has been selected by a body of which they themselves form part—but the feelings of their constituents also have to be taken into account. And hence he states that he hesitated to accept the office of arbitrator, which had been pressed upon him, because of his own connection with the trade. But the success with which he has filled the post upon more than one occasion, and the confidence felt in him by both parties, and especially—although he is an employer—by the men, and expressed through the mouths[161] of their advocates, and shown in actual fact by his appointment as referee to their standing committee,[162] prove that in his case at least the advantages of tried experience have been sufficient to outweigh the probability of suspicions of personal bias. We must not, however, forget that he occupies an unusual position; that he had been a prime mover in the establishment of the board in 1869;[163]

[157] Cf. K, pp. 28 and 37.   [158] Cf. II, p. 5.   [159] Cf. I, p. 5.
[160] Cf. I, p. 3.   [161] Cf. I, p. 18; IV, p. 3; VII, p. 8; VIII, p. 6.
[162] Cf. VI, p. 8; IX, p. 4.   [163] Cf. II, p. 9.

that he had himself acted as President for some years, and "had
"won the confidence of both employers and employed;"[161] and that
in one case at least it seems[165] to have been thought undesirable
by some of the workmen—though not apparently by their representatives—to refer a point to him for decision, because he was
himself "largely interested in the trade."

Nor must we neglect to notice the advantages of securing a
comparative stranger for the office. Thus, in the Northumberland
coal trade, Sir Lyon Playfair states[166] at the conclusion of an arbitration, in which he has been sitting as umpire, that he is a "blank
"sheet at present, except as regards the interesting information"
he has gathered from the discussion; and in the iron trade, Sir
Joseph Pease says[167] in 1882 that he "comes with a very blank
"mind with regard to the whole question." "My mind," he adds,
"is a complete 'tableau recevant,' as the French would say, and
"liable to any impression that can be made upon it." Nor, indeed,
as a matter of fact, is success in the conduct of arbitrations by any
means confined to men actually engaged in the same trade as that
in which they sit as arbitrators, or indeed to those engaged in trade
at all. Sir Rupert Kettle's experience in arbitration has been
of the widest description, and his success has been equally
undoubted,[168] but, according to Mr. Weeks,[169] he has had no
practical knowledge of the iron and coal trades in which he has so
often sat; and Mr. Hughes, Mr. (now Lord) Herschell, Mr. (now
Lord) Brassey, Mr. Crompton, and Mr. Shaw-Lefevre could not
be called experts in trade, and yet they have all been selected as
arbitrators.

The chief difficulties, moreover, involved in the selection of an
outsider can be to some extent overcome. In the first place there is
the necessity of explaining to him such technicalities of the trade as
may be necessary to render intelligible the terminology employed
by either side. In the second place he must be acquainted with
such of the past history of the trade, and of the proceedings at
previous arbitrations, as may enable him to appraise at their
proper value the contentions and arguments of either party. Thus
Sir Rupert Kettle has to be informed[170] by the Northumberland
miners that the underground men are there divided into "hewers"
and "off-hand men," and that the above-ground men are called
"bankmen;" whereas in Staffordshire the latter are termed

    [161] Cf. IV, p. 6.   [165] Cf. IX, pp. 4 and 12.
    [166] Cf. P, p. 131.
    [167] Cf. IV, p. 3; i.e., because he "had been so little engaged in the actual
"detail of iron manufacture, at any rate for a great number of years."
    [168] Cf. II, p. 22, and VI, p. 4.   [169] Cf. Report, sec. x, p. 22.
    [170] Cf. K, p. 17.

" banksmen," and the former are classified as "pikemen" and
" bandmen;" and Lord Herschell has to be told[171] that there are
classes of men employed in and about the mines, who are not connected with the miners' union. And in the iron trade the president, in opening the proceedings of the board before Mr. Watson,
expresses[172] the gist of the matter when he says, "we cannot
" expect him (i.e., Mr. Watson) to be so well acquainted with the
" details of our trade as one who for years has been intimately
" connected with it;" and Mr. Watson himself remarks that this
ignorance may "occasion from time to time some slowness" in the
proceedings. "I shall require," he adds, "an explanation of
" technical terms."

(2). Now these difficulties may possibly be in some measure
avoided by the method generally followed in the Northumberland
and Durham coal trades, by which either party appoints two
arbitrators who are really representative of either side, and
generally possess local knowledge, and these arbitrators select an
umpire who occupies the position of an independent mediator.
Then, as Sir Rupert Kettle puts it,[173] the arbitrators and umpire
form one body of five, and the umpire will only step in if the arbitrators fail to agree. Up to this point he merely lends his assistance
and counsel to the arbitrators who are the primary judges. This
method however does not seem to work with very considerable
success, for the arbitrators, being representative of either side, do
not apparently as a general rule come to an agreement, and the
final award is left to the umpire. In the iron trade the men again
and again express[174] dissatisfaction with the award given by Messrs.
Mundella and Williams, when they sat as arbitrators in 1876. A
workman declares[175] before Mr. Dale in 1877 that they had told Mr.
Mundella that the "award must come from the umpire and not from
" him alone, or from a compromise between him and Mr. Williams."
Mr. Mundella, it seems, had asked the operative members of the
board to authorise him to effect an amicable settlement of the
case, and they had refused; and another of their number maintains[176] before Mr. Watson in 1884 that the arbitrator who represented the masters, Mr. Williams, "contrived to frighten" their
own arbitrator, Mr. Mundella. Nor did Mr. Shaw-Lefevre's award
give greater satisfaction, although in this case the umpire himself,
and not the arbitrators, who were Messrs. Lloyd Jones and Williams,
gave the final decision. The men declare before Mr. Watson that,
although they had no doubt of Mr. Shaw-Lefevre's "integrity," and

---

[171] *Cf.* II, p. 50.
[172] *Cf.* VI, p. 3. [173] *Cf.* K, p. 30; II, p. 14; II, p. 16.
[174] *Cf.* I, pp. 13 and 14, &c. [175] *Cf.* I, p. 14.
[176] *Cf.* VI, p. 11.

loyally adhered to his award, yet they "always felt that had the
" secretaries been permitted to be present with the arbitrators
" before the umpire in January, 1879, the award would have been
" more favourable to the workmen."[177] At any rate they concluded
that the old system of a single arbitrator was the better of the two;
and in 1882, when the question of reference to arbitration arose, we
find[178] that the " operatives expressed themselves strongly in favour
" of a sole arbitrator, as against two arbitrators and an umpire,"
and Mr. J. W. Pease was selected to act in that capacity. These
complaints indeed may be said to have been caused by accidental
circumstances, and not to affect the essence of the system. But
this point is open to question, for there can be little doubt that, if
avowed representatives of opposing parties sit together upon the
same judicial bench, the judgment pronounced must of necessity
partake of the nature of a compromise; and when a dispute has
passed beyond the stage of conciliation and has reached that of
arbitration, additional machinery for effecting a compromise can
hardly be said to be located in its proper place. If on the other
hand the final decision falls to the lot of the umpire, then the
arbitrators might more suitably appear as open advocates than as
" quasi-judges." The system, in short, of two or more arbitrators
and a single umpire, seems to be at the best an unnecessary piece
of mechanism, and the greater the simplicity that can be obtained
in these courts of arbitration, the less will be the expenditure
entailed, and in all probability also the more satisfactory will be
the results achieved. We must not however forget that in some
trades the practice may have become traditional, or may meet with
ready acceptance; and, should this be the case, then on the
principles laid down at the beginning of this report, the inconvenience which seems to follow from the practice would probably
be more than counterbalanced by the advantage of habitual or
approved usage.

But the special difficulty which the practice may perhaps in
some cases meet, seems to be solved in a more satisfactory
manner by retaining, if possible, the services of the same arbitrator time after time. Of course there may be adequate reasons
for making a change, and in the iron trade Mr. Trow argues[179]
that they did not select Mr. Dale as arbitrator in 1882, because
they thought it well to get a " new man," " free from all former
" traditions," to preside at proceedings, which involved "a depar-
" ture from that which for some years" had "governed their
" action." But, save in these exceptional cases, there are manifest
advantages in having the same arbitrator. The president of the
board puts the matter in a nutshell before Mr. Watson, sitting as

[177] Cf. VI, p. 5.   [178] Cf. IV, p. 5.   [179] Cf. IV, p. 3.

ITS ADVANTAGES, METHODS, AND DIFFICULTIES. 53

arbitrator for the second time, in April, 1884, when he says,[180] " we
" shall approach the question to-day as it were with an old friend,
" because we feel that the time we occupied on the last occasion
" was so exceedingly long, that we shall not have to ask him
" (i.e., Mr. Watson) on the present occasion to sit for any length
" of time." In the previous case, when Mr. Watson was acting as
arbitrator for the first time, the past history of the board had to
be laid before him, and a similar course was followed before Mr.
Pease in April, 1882, and Mr. Shaw-Lefevre, in 1878.[181] But
this was not required[182] before Mr. (then Sir Joseph) Pease in
November, 1882, or before Mr. Watson in April or November,
1884, or October, 1885.

(iv) (a). Nor is the avoidance of detail the only advantage connected with the reappointment of the same arbitrator on successive
occasions. But there is another consideration of the highest
importance, and this is stated[183] by Lord Herschell in his award in
the Northumberland coal trade of 31st January, 1876. He
recommends the·adoption of a sliding scale in the trade, and also
the creation of an arbitration-tribunal of a permanent character;
and he argues that in this way " a uniform principle would " " be
" applied," and " justice would more certainly be done to all parties "
than it would if the tribunal were " different on each occasion," and
were " unable to know completely and accurately the principles on
" which its predecessors proceeded." This uncertainty of the basis
on which the award is to rest is perhaps the greatest difficulty
connected with arbitration. Mr. Lloyd Jones, in a paper read
before the Industrial Remuneration Conference, maintained[184] that
arbitration was " slow, expensive, and at the same time very uncer-
" tain in its results;" and he alluded to a possible insufficiency
and inaccuracy of data, and to a suspicion of prejudice in the
mind of the arbitrator. A passage in an article on Trade-
Unionism in the " Co-operative Wholesale Society's Annual "[185] for
1886, puts forward a somewhat similar indictment. Now of course,
if the alternative were to lie between the method of arbitration and
the method of strikes and lock-outs, this objection could hardly be
regarded as valid. For the irritation caused by a strike or lock-
out must in all likelihood be greater and more permanent than the
irritation caused by the decision of an arbitrator, before whom the
contending parties rely upon argument and not upon force. And,
if an arbitrator be liable to error, it may be urged with as much

[180] Cf. VII, p. 3.
[181] Cf. II, p. 6; IV, p. 7; VI, p. 4.   [182] Cf. V, p. 4; VII, p. 3.
[183] Cf. II, p. 240   [184] Cf. I. R. C. Report, p. 33.
[185] Cf. " Co-operative Wholesale Society's Annual," 1886, p. 271. This
difficulty of course applies also to conciliation.

reason that a strike or lock-out is not free from suspicion of
error. Nor indeed, if the idea commonly held that arbitrators'
awards were given by "some splitting of the difference," or
"softening the way," or "making things pleasant,"[186] were strictly
and literally true, could it even in that case be denied that it is
something to soften a feeling of hostility between unfriendly parties,
by referring the dispute to a neutral mediator who is guiltless of
unfriendly feelings, and is consequently able to "make things
"pleasant." But nevertheless, after giving full weight to all these
considerations, there still remains the undoubted fact that there is
this difficulty inherent in arbitration—the difficulty of determining
upon the principle which is to be recognised in the decision of
industrial disputes. The two parties must, as Lord Herschell has
said,[187] "proceed on some principle or other, if it is not to be a
" 'leap in the dark.' "

But this principle can hardly be supplied by Political Economy.
Sir Rupert Kettle,[188] indeed, sitting as arbitrator in the Northumberland coal trade, says that he is a "political economist,"
but he adds that he requires "to go to the root of the matter
"minutely as a man of business," before he gives his judgment.
And, as Jevons[189] has shown in his "Theory of Political Economy,"
in all bargains about a single *indivisible* object "there may arise
"a deadlock," because neither party can read the mind of the
other, and discern the exact length to which it is prepared to
go in pushing demands or accepting concessions. Nor indeed, did
they possess the gift of clairvoyance, would the problem be
necessarily solved. For even then there might be no definite
point fixed in the mind of either. After alluding to this passage in
his "State in Relation to Labour," he proceeds[190] to point out that
the existence of *indivisible* combinations in trade disputes usually
reduces them to a bargain of this "indeterminate" nature. To
avoid a strike it may be the interest of either party to relinquish,
or at least to relax, its demands; but theoretic economics cannot
resolve the problem. It is, in mathematical phraseology, "indeter-
"minate." There is moreover in the case such an element of
extra-economic considerations—of feelings of justice, for example,
or suspicions of "*mala fides*"—that it seems obvious that a trade
dispute—especially when it has reached the "acute" stage of an
open quarrel—"has little or nothing to do with economics." It is
rather to the traditions of the trade and the past history of industrial relations that arbitrators must look for guidance. If then

---

[186] *Cf. supra*, p. 49.   [187] *Cf.* II, p. 71.   [188] *Cf.* K, p. 37.
[189] *Cf.* "Theory of Political Economy," by W. S. Jevons, 2nd edit.,
pp. 130—137.
[190] *Cf.* "State in Relation to Labour," p. 154, &c.

there have been previous arbitrations, reference to them is almost necessitated, for " it would " " be the height of presumption " " to " ignore the labour of those who have previously been consulted " by both parties."[191] Should the precedents, however, appear to conflict, an additional element of difficulty is imported into the matter—the difficulty of determining which precedent ought to be allowed the greatest validity. But this difficulty is evidently reduced to the smallest dimensions if the arbitrator on successive occasions is the same individual, for he naturally adheres to his own precedents, and tends in this way to establish a permanent tradition.

(b). The difficulties of this nature arising in arbitrations may be roughly divided into two classes, although the separation is to a certain extent artificial. In the first place there is the difficulty of deciding upon the data which are to be taken into consideration as a basis for the arbitrator's award; and in the second place there is the additional difficulty of ascertaining these data with accurate exactitude. This will be more clearly apparent if we consider some illustrative instances.

Let us take, for example, the three arbitration reports of the Northumberland coal trade, and the nine arbitration reports of the manufactured iron trade of the North, to which previous reference has been made; and let us notice some of the leading arguments which have been adduced on successive occasions.

(c) (1). In the case of the Northumberland coal trade there is an agreement of tolerable uniformity with regard to the general character of the data on which the decision is to be based. " Both " parties," remarks Lord Herschell in his award of 1876, " are " pretty well agreed that the change of prices must mainly be the " basis in determining what changes should be made in wages."[192]

The owners, in their written case before Sir Rupert Kettle in 1875, " unhesitatingly deny "[193] that the award " shall be based " upon a question of profits," because, they say, labour would thus share in profits without sharing in losses, and because the " price " of labour really and truly depends upon supply and demand, " and cannot legitimately be governed by any other law." " To a " certain extent," indeed, they urge, the same objections apply to the basis of prices; but " there seems to be a sort of recognised " feeling shared by employers and employed," with which " the " public at large scarcely agree," " that the price of an article may " be used as a rough, unskilful, but practical mode of settling the " question between capital and labour." And hence they accept

" this mode of dealing with the question " as an " expedient "—
though only as an " expedient "—and they base their demand for a
reduction in wages upon the fact " that the wages-cost of producing
" coal has risen in a greater degree than that in which prices have
" advanced;" and the previous mutual arrangements, to which they
refer in detail, seem to have rested upon a similar basis.[194] Before
Lord Herschell they " are content to let " the basis of prices
" rest," for " though an unskilful, it is a rough and practical mode
" which, in the hands of experienced arbitrators, may perhaps be
" the least objectionable way of dealing with all the difficulties
" which surround the subject."[195] And in this instance again they
rest the burden of their case upon the basis of selling prices. On
the third occasion, before Sir Lyon Playfair, they once more
allude[196] to a decline in prices as one reason at least for a reduction
in wages.

The men on their part cordially accept this basis. " As a matter
" of fact," they urge, " this has been the basis accepted by both
" sides during all the negotiations relative to wages of late
" years."[197] " For our part, although we are far from believing
" that it is a perfect method, and firmly hold indeed that profits
" and losses are an important element in the question, and that
" these should always be taken into the account, we yet trust that
" our present system will only be abandoned when we see our way
" to the adoption of a better, more equitable, and more satisfactory
" method of adjusting our differences." " The only principle on
" which both parties seem to be agreed or—whether agreed or
" not—on which they have practically acted hitherto, both in the
" advances and reductions of recent years, is the relation between
" price and wages."[198] " We have always expressed our readiness
" to have wages regulated by the prices received for the coal, and
" we have shown our confidence in this principle, and our readiness
" to abide by it, by adhering to it not only when the markets
" were rising, but also since they began to fall."[199] " We will only
" say now " (in answer to the point of declining prices advanced
by the owners) " that whatever fall can be proved to have taken
" place in the price of coal since last arbitration, will be acknow-
" ledged by us as a reason for a reduction in wage, provided that
" all other matters are allowed for on our side as they have
" hitherto been on the side of employers in past arbitrations."[200]
' In all our previous arbitrations this " (fall in prices) " has been
" the ground selected by the owners, and we fail to see why they
" should now import other matters into the case, and seek a wholly

[194] Cf. K, pp. 3, 6, 8, 11.   [195] Cf. H, p. 7.
[196] Cf. P. p. 7.   [197] Cf. K, p. 49.
[198] Cf. H, p. 23.   [199] Cf. H, p. 25.   [200] Cf. P, p. 19.

" new basis to work upon."[201] "We have always recognised the
" principle of wages rising and falling with the prices received by
" the coal-owners."[202]

(2). But other considerations besides the bare relation of the
figures of wages to the *figures* of prices are, as a matter of fact,
introduced into the different cases. It is difficult to distinguish
exactly between the amount of expenses of production which is to
be charged to wages,—if we do not rest content with the mere
numerical statement of the total sum actually received by the
workmen—and the amount which is to be charged to other
elements; and hence in this, if in no other way, some other
elements are almost of necessity introduced into the arguments
of the one side or the other.

Let us take, for an illustration of this, the arbitration at which
Sir Rupert Kettle presided in March, 1875. The accountants
appointed to examine the books have, according to the owners[203]
taken into consideration only the "amount of wage paid in
" bringing coal to bank." But the owners allude in their case[204]
to the increased cost occasioned by the effect of the Mines
Regulation Act, which came into force in the year 1873, and of
the Nine-hours' movement of the year 1871, upon the number of
working hours in a week. They also refer to the augmented
number of "hewers" and to the consequent increase in the
cottages and fuel provided for their accommodation, and in the
time expended in taking them up and down the pits. The miners
reply[205] to this by saying that it is unfair to charge them with the
cost, direct or indirect, entailed by beneficial legislation; and that
the argument about the diminution of working hours is met by the
fact that the miners are paid, not by time, but by the amount of
coal that they respectively "send to bank." In answer to this the
employers point[206] to the "standing charges"—"such as house-
" rent, fire-coal, horses, plant and machinery," and the fixed wages
paid to certain classes of workmen—and they contend that these
" charges are constant," whether the "hewers" are working or
not; and this the miners "readily admit."[207] The mere relation,
then, of the figures of wages to the figures of prices does not seem
to be fully accepted by the owners.

---

[201] *Cf.* P, p. 26.   [202] *Cf.* P, p. 27.

[203] *Cf.* K, p. 13 ; or, more fully, " the actual lump sum of money paid at each
" colliery for hewing and bringing the coal to bank," *together with* " the cost of
" extra cottage accommodation required." " The average net price per ton "
which the " coal cost the owners in wages " is thus compared with the " average
" net price per ton " at which the coals were sold " at the pit's mouth." *Cf.* K,
p. 11.

[204] *Cf.* K, p. 7.   [205] *Cf.* K, p. 45.   [206] *Cf.* K, p. 93.

[207] *Cf.* K, p. 115.

The men on their part contend that they can only be credited
with the advance of wages which they (*i.e.*, the hewers) have
actually obtained.[208] But they also maintain[209] that it is "altogether
" unjust to throw the whole burden of all increased cost in wages
" on the shoulders of the workmen." They allude, for example, to
the difficulty of working " thinner and harder seams "—although
the facts they adduce upon this point are contested by the owners.
They urge that, to produce the same amount of coal, these seams
require a greater number of hands, whether of the " hewers "
themselves or of the "off-hand men "[210] or labourers, who have to
" make height for the ponies and to keep the roadways in proper
" order." As the workings extend further from the shaft the " cost
" of labour for the transit of the coal " must also be increased ; and
these " natural disadvantages of working," they claim, ought not to
be charged against them. Nor, if the whole of the increased cost
of *wages* is to fall on their shoulders, is the " injustice " avoided of
crediting them with the expense entailed by errors of management
in applying and directing labour. For in recent years alone
the owners in their anxiety to augment production had "imported"
" great numbers " of " untrained hands" into the mines.

Nor is the other element of price allowed by the arbitrator to
rest upon the mere figures ; for he addresses a question to[211] either
side with the object of ascertaining whether there had been any
alteration in the quality of the coal sold; and in his award he
states[212] that some difference was discovered "in the relative
" proportions of the yield of 'round' and 'small' coal," "at the
" two test periods,"[213] "which affected to a small extent the
" average selling value of the (unit) ton of coal." The direct
comparison, then, of the figures of wages with the figures of
prices does not seem to be fully accepted by either party before
Sir Rupert Kettle.

Nor is this condition of affairs materially altered before Lord
Herschell or Sir Lyon Playfair. For the men again contend[214]
before Lord Herschell, that the "cost of wages " is a misleading
expression ; and that they ought not to be credited with the
expense entailed by "natural disadvantages and difficulties," by
official " carelessness and mismanagement," or by "special privi-

---

[208] *Cf.* K, p. 53.   [209] *Cf.* K, p. 51.
[210] The general statements of the accountants are supplemented during the
course of the arbitration by detailed percentages, giving separately the increase in
the average earnings of the "hewers," and in those of the " off-hand men," and
the " mechanics," &c.   *Cf.* K, pp. 98 and 99.
[211] *Cf.* K, p. 90.   [212] *Cf.* K, p. 121.
[213] And also " some slight difference in the average thickness of the seams
" working at the two " periods. *Cf.* K, p. 121.
[214] *Cf.* H, p. 26; P, p. 103.

" leges," or " higher salaries " granted to particular classes of workmen who are not members of the Miners' Association. They also
institute a comparison between their own position and that of the
miners in other districts ;[215] and the owners in their case before
Sir Lyon Playfair,[216] follow in the same line, calling special
attention to the fact that it is the peculiar practice in Durham and
Northumberland to supply the colliers with houses and fuel. With
regard to prices, again, the difficulty of disposing of the "small"
coal, is urged[217] before Sir Lyon Playfair, and is described in his
award as the "chief element" in the arbitration.

(3). But, even if the general character of the data on which the
award is to be based is determined, the difficulties are not thereby
entirely resolved. For these data have to be ascertained with accuracy. The information, for example, obtained by the two parties
with reference to the comparison of the position of the miners in
Northumberland with that of the men in other districts seems to
have been of so conflicting a nature that the point was abandoned
by mutual consent before Lord Herschell ;[218] and, before Sir Lyon
Playfair, one of the representatives of the men remarks :[219] "It has
" been stated again and again that it is almost impossible to get
" the wages of hewers in other districts " (i.e., besides Durham).
He affirms that he has data which are entirely contrary to those
furnished by the owners, and that, in addition to this, the nature of
the work in other districts is very different from that in Northumberland. Finally the owners abandon comparison with any other
districts save that of Durham alone,[220] and with that they only
compare a "portion" of Northumberland ; but even to this the
miners object[221] by urging that Durham "contains every variety of
" coal, and a great number of different seams," and that, to make
the comparison "in any degree fair and relevant, collieries of a
" similar kind, working the same seams, exactly under the same
" circumstances, and sending their coal to the same market, should
" alone be compared." Nor, if we turn to other elements in the
expenses of production besides wages, is any information at all to
be procured ; for the owners stoutly deny that profits have any
concern in the matter, and emphatically refuse to supply evidence
about the expenses of management.[222]

But, supposing that the basis of selling prices, as contrasted
with the cost of wages, is accepted as suitable and fair : here also
difficulties arise. The owners, indeed, permit chartered accountants,
sworn to secrecy, to inspect their books. Before Sir Rupert Kettle

---

[215] *Cf.* II, p. 22.
[216] *Cf.* P, pp. 9—11.   [217] *Cf.* P, pp. 8, 133, and 134.
[218] *Cf.* II, p. 165.   [219] *Cf.* P, pp. 21 and 74.   [220] *Cf.* P, p. 83.
[221] *Cf.* P, p. 120.   [222] *Cf.* P, p. 42.

they produce a statement drawn up by the accountants, and a letter describing the method which had been followed in obtaining the figures;[223] and this statement is accepted[224] by the men as "arithmetically" correct. Before Lord Herschell, indeed, they ask[225] that the figures presented by the owners,—and obtained in this instance through the agency of the "ordinary staff" of their association—shall be verified by accountants nominated by the umpire; and this course is actually followed. But the "arithme-"tical accuracy" of the figures, when verified by accountants,[226] is acknowledged as a fair basis on which to proceed; for, as Sir Rupert Kettle puts it,[227] "the figures are taken from books kept "quite independently of" the "arbitration by clerks who have no "other interest in them than the receipt of their salaries; and the "tables are copied from the books, and these books are examined "by public accountants who, if they are worth their salt, are like "a two-foot rule."

The principle, however, on which they are based may be open to objection. For the men can only obtain detailed information with the "utmost difficulty." "The employer has ready at his "command all the data in the shape of books, documents, and "figures requisite for the preparation of his case,"[228] but the miner is in this respect placed at a great disadvantage. The figures submitted by the accountants are necessarily given in averages or percentages, because the owners do not wish to render the public— and still less their rival traders—acquainted with the details of the inner working of their business.[229] But the objection to this course is fairly stated[230] by one of the workmen's advocates, when he urges before Lord Herschell that, if he knew the figures of particular collieries, he might be able to "thoroughly investigate" the matter, and insert in his reply "some statement in relation to "it which might modify" some of the figures put in, and account for the increased cost occurring in special cases.

The method, also, of uniting and separating the several percentages may undergo variation; and in this way a fresh element of difficulty in comparing the figures of the present with those of the past may be introduced. Thus in the figures supplied to Sir Rupert Kettle contracts were not included,[231] but in those supplied to Lord Herschell the contrary course was adopted, and objection is taken to this by the umpire[232] on the ground that it prevents exact

[223] Cf. K, pp. 10 and 11.
[224] Cf. K, p. 55.   [225] Cf. II, pp. 2, 7, 21, and 236.
[226] Cf. K, p. 58.   [227] Cf. K, p. 26.   [228] Cf. K, p. 43.
[229] Cf. II, p. 9, &c.; cf. also K, pp. 27 and 28.
[230] Cf. II, pp. 15 and 220.
[231] Cf. K, p. 10.   [232] Cf. II, p. 33.

comparison. In the former case, again, a distinction was made between the men working in the "soft-coal collieries" and those in the "steam-coal collieries," and a special reduction demanded in the case of the former; and Lord Herschell insists[233] that a similar distinction ought to be made before him in the returns of selling prices; for otherwise the result of an average may be to injure the relative position of the workmen at one class of colliery to the benefit of those at another. A further question is raised before him with reference to the separation of the increased cost of wages due to members of the Miners' Association from that due to outsiders;[234] for, if the wages of the one class be maintained in adverse times at the point they reached in prosperity, it would apparently be unfair to charge the whole increase in the relative cost of wages to the other class. But in this instance, as in that of the question of contracts, the difference resulting from inclusion or exclusion was shown to be only about 1 per cent.[235] Lastly, it was argued before the same arbitrator that certain collieries in connection with the Masters' Association produced clay and other commodities besides coal, and that the cost incurred when the men were producing clay ought to be excluded from the calculated cost of wages, if the selling price only of coal entered into the calculated prices;[236] but this objection, the owners reply, had been met by taking account of the sales of clay in the calculations of prices.

(4). When these difficulties about the accuracy of the data placed before the arbitrator have been resolved, there remains yet another of very considerable importance. For it is evident that, if wages are to be regulated by selling prices, there must be some agreement with regard to the time when the two are to be considered as standing in a normal relation towards one another. Thus before Sir Rupert Kettle the owners instituted a comparison between the month of January, 1875, and the month of April, 1871; and it seems to have been generally acknowledged by the men that April, 1871, was properly chosen as a test month, representing, in the words of the arbitrator, the "normal condition "of rate of wages and price of commodity in the coal trade."[237] But Sir Rupert Kettle himself held[238] that the month of January, 1875, was an abnormal period in these respects; and the men protest[239] before Lord Herschell against the fairness of the comparison. They argue, indeed, for general reasons that in view of

---

[233] *Cf.* II, p. 39. [234] *Cf.* II, pp. 27, 41—59.
[235] *Cf.* II, p. 181. [236] *Cf.* II, pp. 61—63.
[237] *Cf.* K, pp. 69, 71, 95, and 121. [238] *Cf.* K, p. 123.
[239] *Cf.* II, p. 28. April, 1871, is also now regarded by the men as an abnormal period, because two days more than the average were worked per week. *Cf.* II, p. 80.

the "fluctuations in the coal trade" a single month is not an adequately broad and reliable basis for such a comparison.[210] But, even accepting this narrow basis, they point out that, whereas in the month of April the "Baltic trade" is "opened out," "the "month of January is usually one of the worst in the year," both from the dulness of trade and the prevalence of holiday festivities. And hence the comparison pressed unfairly upon the men in two ways. It raised "the average price," and lessened the "propor- "tionate cost of wages in April, 1871." It lowered the average price, and increased the cost in January, 1875. The justice of this contention is admitted by the arbitrator; and the investigations made by the accountants which he appointed to inquire into the matter showed[211] that, comparing November, 1875, with April, 1871, there was an increase of 74 per cent. in the wages-cost, but that, comparing the same month with January, 1871, there was only an increase of 57½ per cent., although the prices in the two months of January and April were about the same. And hence it is evident that these peculiar circumstances must be borne in mind in estimating the fair and normal relation of wages to prices, and in instituting comparisons between one period and another.

(d) (1). Throughout the nine reports, again, in the manufac- tured iron trade, there is a general agreement that the basis of the award is to be primarily the relation of wages to selling prices. But the agreement is not uniformly maintained, and a number of additional considerations are advanced. The table which is given in an earlier portion of this report[212] affords evidence of a general correspondence between selling prices and puddling wages, and the fact is noticed by more than one arbitrator,[213] by Mr. Dale, for instance, in 1879, and by Sir Joseph Pease in 1882. The very existence of sliding scales in the trade on four separate occasions is proof of a tendency to adopt this relation as a basis. The masters appeal[214] to the evidence of prices before Mr. Dale in 1877, Mr. Shaw-Lefevre in 1878, Mr. Dale again in 1879, Sir Joseph Pease in 1882, and Mr. Watson in 1884 and 1885, and in fact rest the chief burden of their cases upon this. "It is quite impossible," their advocate maintains[215] before Mr. Dale in 1879, " if wages do " not in some degree comport with" the "market price, for us to " carry on our business successfully." Before Sir Joseph Pease he alludes[216] to "the eight years' settlements based on the selling price " of iron," and he adds these words: "The eight years' sliding

[210] Cf. II, p. 74.   [211] Cf. II, p. 237.
[212] Cf. supra, p 21.   [213] Cf. III, p. 14; IV, p. 24.
[214] Cf. I, p. 5; II, p. 3; III, p. 9; IV, p. 10; V, p. 5; VI, p. 4; VII, p. 3; VIII, p. 3; IX, p. 4.
[215] Cf. III, p. 11.   [216] Cf. IV, p. 12.

" scale arrangement, we believe, was the principle of determining
" wages by the selling price of iron, and it would be extremely
" difficult, if not dangerous, permanently to depart from that."
The men on their part recognise the same general basis. Before
Mr. Dale in 1877 they argue[247] that " the selling price of iron does
" not justify the employers in demanding any reduction." " As
" our wages in the past," they urge, " have been regulated by
" the selling price of iron and not by the condition of trade, we
" protest against the plea of depression being used for the purpose
" of reducing our wages, and maintain that we have a right to
" claim that our wages shall now be regulated on the former
" basis, viz., selling price of iron, and not on the state of
" trade." " We entirely agree that our wages should be regulated
" by the selling price of iron."[248] " We have a right to demand
" that a full inquiry shall be made, and that our wages shall only
" be ruled by the former basis, viz., the selling price of iron."
And they warmly protest[249] against the award of Messrs. Mundella
and Williams on the ground that it was given on a new basis—on
the depression of trade. But on the other hand the suspension of
the sliding scales is evidence of an unwillingness to abide entirely
by the changes in selling prices; and the men, in the very case to
which we have just alluded—that before Mr. Dale in 1877—say[250]
that " it is not always fair to base wages on the price of the article
" produced." Before Sir Joseph Pease in 1882 they maintain[251]
that the " value of their labour, in addition to the selling price,
" had been recognised " (with one exception) from the formation
of the board in 1869 until September, 1873; that in that and the
following year the employers made the utmost use of the surplus
of labour in the market; that in 1875 it was the state of the labour
market that gave the employers the advantage, and enabled them
to effect a reduction; and that now in 1882 the men ought in
their turn to reap the fruits of the comparative scarcity of labour.
Before Mr. Watson in 1884 they protest[252] against following prices
down to their lowest point, and argue that in the days of prosperity they did not follow them up to the highest point.

The condition, then, of the labour market, as well as the position
of wages relative to prices, is urged by the men upon the attention
of arbitrators. The reduction of $7\frac{1}{2}$ per cent. effected by mutual
arrangement at Birmingham in December, 1873, was expressly
agreed to by the operatives. according to the contention[253] of their
advocate, Mr. Trow, before Sir Joseph Pease in 1882, because of
their knowledge of the congested condition of the labour market.

[247] Cf. I, p. 5.   [248] Cf. I, pp. 15 and 23.
[249] Cf. I, p. 17.   [250] Cf. I, p. 8.   [251] Cf. IV, p. 7.
[252] Cf. VIII, p. 5.   [253] Cf. IV, p. 10.

The success of the board is attributed[254] by them on the same
occasion to the fact that in its early history " each arbitrator dealt
" with the question submitted not on a narrow basis, but took a
" broad view, and gave awards in accordance with the value of
" labour and the conditions of the labour market at the time of
" the sitting." Sir Joseph Pease once more, in his award on the
same occasion, sums up their objections[255] to the exclusive basis
of selling prices, and notices that an additional fact in support of
their contention had been brought into the light during the course
of the inquiry—the fact that certain allowances under the names of
" prize money " and " Monday working money " were " freely
" given during times of scarcity in the labour market," and
" immediately withdrawn by certain employers " when the conditions of that market inclined in their favour.

Somewhat akin to the condition of the labour market is another
consideration which has had no little weight from time to time in
the history of the board. This is the relative position of the
ironworkers in the north of England as compared with that of
the Staffordshire men. The sliding scale of 1871 was suspended
because the rates in Staffordshire were raised above those given
by the scale in the north of England. The Staffordshire men
obtained an advance of 20 per cent. The sliding scale in the
north gave an advance only of $7\frac{1}{2}$ per cent.[256] The scale was
suspended, and an immediate advance of $12\frac{1}{2}$ per cent. accorded.
The Derby scale of 1874 was the result of a joint arrangement
between the employers and employed of the north and of Staffordshire. The average selling price under this scale was to be
ascertained[257] by an examination into the books of all the firms in
the north of England and of twelve selected firms in Staffordshire.
The average selling prices of the one were to be added to those of
the other and divided by two, and the result of this calculation
was to be the price recognised by the scale. Mr. Shaw-Lefevre's
award, again, was apparently[258] based in a considerable degree upon
the Staffordshire wages. Men and masters both appeal[259] before
him to the Staffordshire rates and to the wages of the ironworkers
in other districts as well; and this same standard of comparison is
invoked on more than one other occasion.[260] The relative position,
also, of ironworkers as compared with the men engaged in other
trades finds a place in some of the arguments both of masters and

254 *Cf.* IV, p. 15.   255 *Cf.* IV, p. 23.
256 *Cf.* II, p. 6.
257 *Cf.* I, p. 11; II, p. 10.
258 *Cf.* II, p. 19; III, pp. 10 and 11.   *Cf. contra*, VI, p. 9.
259 *Cf.* II, pp. 3 and 6; III, p. 11; IV, p. 8.
260 *Cf.* I, pp. 10 and 11; IV, p. 10; VIII, p. 9.

of men ;[261] and another contention advanced upon some occasions is indirectly connected with this.

Thus the men appeal before[262] Mr. Dale in 1877 to the fact that a diminution in the expenses of production has been occasioned by a fall in the prices of pig iron and of coal, and consequently urge that a reduction in selling prices does not necessarily imply a decrease in profits; and the masters admit that this contention is one of considerable strength if supported by actual facts, and do not call in question at the moment the accuracy of the figures put in by the men with regard to the prices of pig iron and coal. But they argue[263] that the workers in the manufactured iron trade have not contributed towards these reductions; that the Durham colliers have had their wages decreased on three occasions since the last award in the manufactured iron trade; that the cokemen have undergone a similar process, and so have the colliery mechanics and engine-men. Reductions have also been effected in the wages of the Cleveland ironstone miners and in those of the blast furnace-men. And so the cost of other items in the expenses of production over and beyond the cost of labour is urged upon the attention of arbitrators.[264] The men advance this consideration on the occasion to which we have just referred, and the masters admit that it is a " strong argument."[265] The masters urge the same consideration[266] upon Sir Joseph Pease in 1882; but in this case the men contend that they have "nothing to do" with the cost of material, and that Sir Rupert Kettle on a previous occasion[267] had ruled that it had "no bearing upon" the wages question, although the employers had based the chief burden of their argument for a reduction of wages on the high rates of coal and iron.

But on their part they maintain that a searching inquiry ought to be made into all the details of management, and that the results of careless or incapable direction of industry ought not to be charged to their account;[268] and they urge before Mr. Watson in 1885 that relief should be sought by the employers in diminished royalties and lessened railway rates rather than in decreased wages.[269] The employers, however, emphatically refuse[270] to allow investigation into the inner working of their business with the object of ascertaining the causes of profit or loss; although indeed on their side they appeal more than once to depression in trade as an argument for reduction in wages. The decline[271] in

[261] Cf. I, p. 10; II, p. 15; IV, p. 11; V, p. 10.
[262] Cf. I, p. 7.   [263] Cf. I, p. 11.   [264] Cf. I, p. 11; VII, p. 8.
[265] Cf. I, pp. 7, 9, and 16.   [266] Cf. V, pp. 5 and 7.
[267] October, 1873, at Durham. Cf. IV, pp. 9 and 10; and also at Saltburn in April, 1873; cf. IV, p. 10.
[268] Cf. I, p. 7; II, p. 8; IV, p. 16; IX, p. 14.
[269] Cf. IX, pp. 5, 14 and 15.   [270] Cf. I, p. 9.   [271] Cf. I, p. 5.

F

the demand for iron is impressed upon Mr. Dale in 1877; the "great depression in the manufactured iron trade" is advanced before Mr. Shaw-Lefevre in 1878,[272] and again before Mr. Dale in 1879;[272] and the abandonment of the joint sliding scale in 1875 is justified[273] on the ground of the "great depression in the rail " trade." The men, on the other hand, stoutly protest against the award of Messrs. Mundella and Williams because this plea of depression of trade was taken into consideration; and they maintain that the loss of the rail trade is no concern of theirs, but is " one of those risks to which every capitalist is liable when he " embarks on an industry so precarious and liable to fluctuation as " the iron trade."[274]

There is one other argument of some importance which appears in the arbitration reports from time to time; and this is in one respect at least analogous to the question of profit and loss. For if the men have nothing to do with the "details of manage-" ment," which are the private concerns of the employers, it may be similarly argued, from one point of view, that the employers have nothing to do with those details of household expenditure which are the private concerns of the men. The argument is, however, scarcely sound, and as a matter of fact both employers and men have appealed to what is closely connected with the details of household expenditure—the cost of living or the purchasing power of money. The men allude to the cost of living[275] before Mr. Shaw-Lefevre in 1878; and, in arguing upon the relation of wages to selling prices, they insist that there should be a minimum below which wages should not fall, whatever may be the position of prices.[276] The masters maintain,[277] with considerable detail, in November, 1884, and October, 1885, that the purchasing power of money has increased.

Here then we have a numerous list of arguments advanced on different occasions, in addition to the bare relation of wages to selling prices—the condition of the labour market; the wages paid to ironworkers in Staffordshire and elsewhere, and to men employed in other industries; the additional elements over and above wages in the expenses of production (including the cost of materials, and the amount of royalties and of railway rates); the character of the management of business undertakings; the depression in the demand for iron; and the cost of living. Some of these considerations, of course, have been disallowed on different occasions by the opposing parties, and may or may not have affected

[272] Cf. II, p. 3; III. p. 9.   [273] Cf. I, p. 11.
[274] Cf. I, p. 6.   [275] Cf. II, p. 4.
[276] Cf. I, pp. 8 and 15.
[277] Cf. VII, p. 10; VIII, pp. 10 and 11; IX, p. 11.

the final award; but the fact remains that they have been advanced as data deserving attention.

(2). There is, again, some difficulty experienced in ascertaining these data with exactitude. It is by no means easy to gauge with accuracy the depression of trade, or the conditions of the labour market. The details of management are a closed book, so far as the operatives are concerned; and they can only rely upon the roseate reports of the directors of joint-stock companies.[278] The purchasing power of money is ascertained by the masters from the prices supplied to them by officials connected with the Middles-brough Co-operative Society,[279] but the men contend[280] that they do not "deal with co-operative stores;" that they "live on the "credit system," and that therefore "25 per cent." must be added to co-operative prices before they can fairly be put in as evidence. The comparison of the rates in the north of England with those in Staffordshire is somewhat complicated[281] by the special "extras" which appear to be paid in the former case; but an additional allowance of 6d. in favour of Staffordshire seems to be generally made in calculations of wages. There appears however to have been some irregularity in the payment of these so-called "north-"country extras."[282] The amount of selling prices, on the other hand, is regularly ascertained by the accountant to the board; and this evidence is generally, though not indeed invariably, accepted without question by masters and men.[283] The provision under which these prices are ascertained dates back to the year 1872,[284] and the first quarter for which the accountant's returns were made out was that ending on 29th February in that year. The method pursued by him is described by the president of the board before Mr. Watson in 1884. The figures, he states,[285] are "arrived at by " the examination of the books of all the firms connected with the " board, and also of several others," by Mr. Waterhouse, the accountant to the board. "He takes out and verifies for the two " months' period, and he takes off from the invoices the discounts " and commissions which have to be given by the firms on each " special order, and he arrives at the net price of each ton which " has left the works. And adding these two together, he finds " exactly the total number of tons sold, delivered, and invoiced by " all the firms in the north of England connected with the board. " He gives these figures in certificated returns every two months. " He sends round to the works, and he examines the books himself,

[278] Cf. IX, p. 14.   [279] Cf. VIII, p. 11; IX, p. 11.
[280] Cf. VIII, p. 13.   [281] Cf. II, pp. 7, 12, and 15.
[282] Cf. II, p. 13 and 16; IV, p. 8; V, p. 7; VIII, pp. 11 and 14; IX, p. 6.
[283] Cf. contra, IX, pp. 5 and 9.   [284] Cf. I, p. 18.
[285] Cf. VI, p. 7.

" or by his officials, and vouches for them and their accuracy."
" Every ton of iron of any quality that has been sold by any
" employer " is included in these returns ;[286] and by a mutual agreement effected at Durham in March, 1883, the period of ascertainment was reduced from three to two months, in order to secure
the more rapid adjustment of wages to the changes in prices.

The two following tables will supply illustrations of the
character of these returns :—

TABLE II.[287]

Description.	Quarter ending 29th February, 1872.		
	Weight Invoiced.	Percentage of Total.	Average Net Price per Ton.
	Tons. cwt. qr. lb.		£ s. d.
Rails	71,639 1 3 2	49·35	6 18 1·66
Plates	43,268 4 3 19	29·80	9 4 6·68
Bars	14,398 13 — 27	9·92	7 19 0·89
Angles	15,869 14 1 12	10·93	8 — 7·99
Total	145,175 14 1 4	100·00	7 16 6·15

The second table[288] is given in the employers' case before
Mr. Shaw-Lefevre in December, 1878, and is founded on
Mr. Waterhouse's returns; but rails are omitted, "as they have
" ceased to be an element of any consequence in the iron trade of
" the north of England."

TABLE III.

	18th January, 1876. Williams and Mundella.	Three Months ending 31st August, 1878.	Fall per Ton.	
	£ s. d.	£ s. d.	£ s. d.	
Plates ...	8 — 10·75	6 4 10·29	1 16 0·46 — 17½ ⎫	per cent.
Bars	7 17 9·73	6 1 4·37	1 16 5·36 — 17½ ⎬	reduction
Angles ...	7 13 11·38	5 10 8·43	2 3 2·95 — 22½ ⎭	

Sometimes, however, the prices likely to be realised in the
current or succeeding period, and not those actually realised for
the previous period, have been put in as evidence, and then an
element of uncertainty is at once introduced.[289]

Thus, before Mr. Hughes in January, 1871, the quoted prices,
as given by the "Iron and Coal Trades' Review," were brought

[286] Cf. VII, pp. 5 and 6.
[287] Cf. I, p. 18.   [288] Cf. II, p. 3.
[289] Cf. II, p. 7; V, p. 11.

forward by the employers, but the returns for the six months
following that date indicated a considerable difference from these,
and may be illustrated by the following table, which is based upon
figures supplied by the men to Mr. Shaw-Lefevre in December,
1878.[290]

TABLE IV.

Description.	" Iron and Coal Trades' Review."	Returns for Six Months.
	£ s. d. £ s. d.	£ s. d.
Rails	5 17 6 to 6 - -	6 6 2
Plates	7 7 6 „ 7 10 -	8 4 2
Bars	6 7 6 „ 6 10 -	6 17 6
Angles	6 12 6 „ 6 15 -	7 - 3

(3). The difficulty, once more, of agreeing upon a definite period
when wages are to be considered to bear a normal relation to prices
is again and again brought into clear relief in the manufactured iron
trade. The employers place before successive arbitrators tables
giving the history of the changes in wages between the award of
Messrs. Mundella and Williams in 1876, and the suspension of the
sliding scale in February, 1882; and, if they do not adopt the year
1876 as a starting point, they go back to the Derby scale of 1874.[291]
But the men take objection to this standard on more than one
ground. They declare that it is an unfair basis on which to calculate
the average normal relation of wages to prices. For they maintain[292]
that the award of Messrs. Mundella and Williams cannot be
allowed to enter into the question, as the decision was based not
upon selling prices but upon the novel and dangerous foundation
of depression of trade; and the arbitrators themselves stated both
in the written award—and in the case of Mr. Mundella in a letter
addressed[293] to Mr. Trow, the workmen's representative, in answer
to a definite inquiry upon the point—that the reduction in wages
was not to be considered as " establishing any relative rate of wages
" to prices." Nor, they contend, does Mr. Dale's award of April, 1878,
have any real bearing upon the case, because in all probability,[294]
like that of Mr. Shaw-Lefevre's[295] of 1879, it was based upon the relative position of the wages in other districts and not upon selling
prices. At any rate, they urge, he did not by his award express[296]
any approval of the rate established by that of Messrs. Mundella and
Williams, for he virtually awarded a higher rate than they had

[290] Cf. II, p. 7.
[291] Cf. I, p. 5; II, p. 3; III, p. 9; IV, p. 10; V, p. 6; VI, p. 3.
[292] Cf. I, pp. 6 and 7; IV, pp. 8 and 16.   [293] Cf. III, p. 13.
[294] Cf. II, p. 6; IV, p. 8; V, p. 9; VI, p. 5.
[295] Cf. III, p. 10; VI, pp. 5 and 18; VIII, p. 7.
[296] Cf. VI, p. 5.

done, and he pursued a similar policy in refusing to alter the rate
of wages in August, 1877, and September, 1879. The sliding scale
of 1879, and the Durham arrangement of 1883, are considered by
the men to be unfair ; to have been accepted, partly because of
very important concessions accompanying them ;[297] and to make no
allowance for [298] the 5 per cent. which is generally admitted to be the
value of a time bargain in wages to the employers.[299] The basis
adopted in the Derby sliding scale was, they argue, forced upon
them owing to the state of the labour market,[300] and the reduction
which followed upon its suspension was occasioned by a similar
cause. If then an appeal is to be made to the past history of the
board in order to discover the proper relation of wages to prices,
the whole of that history should be taken into account,[301] and the
times when 2s. 6d. and 2s. 9d., and even 4s. above shillings for
pounds were given should affect the average struck as much as the
depressed times[302] of the Mundella-Williams award or the times of
the 1s. 6d. or 9d. scale. But the employers reply to this by
denouncing such references to the past as appeals[303] to "Old
"Testament history," and "ancient" epochs ; and by maintaining
that the decline, or rather the disappearance,[304] of the rail trade
revolutionised the character of the manufactured iron industry, and
necessitated the abandonment of the arrangement with Staffordshire ; that the average of 1s. 6d. over shillings, fluctuating between
a minimum of 9d. and a maximum of 1s. 9d., has prevailed for a
long period, and is a fair and normal relation ;[305] that, in striking
the average, the times of abnormal and exaggerated prosperity
should be excluded ;[306] that the awards of Messrs. Mundella and
Williams, and of Mr. Shaw-Lefevre, were made after long and
patient and exhaustive inquiry, and were based in the main upon
selling prices, although other matters may also have been taken
into consideration ;[307] that Mr. Dale's awards tended if anything to
confirm that of Messrs. Mundella and Williams, and probably
inclined in favour of the men ;[308] and finally, that the figure of

---

[297] *Cf.* VI, p. 13.
[298] *Cf.* V, p. 9 ; VI, p. 6 ; VIII, p. 12 ; IX, p. 5.
[299] *Cf.* VI, pp. 4 and 14 ; VII, p. 4.
[300] *Cf.* III, p. 10 ; IV, pp. 7, 8, 10, 11 and 16 ; V, p. 9 ; VI, p. 4.
[301] *Cf.* III, p 13 ; V, p. 9 ; VI, p. 4.   [302] *Cf.* IV, p. 16.
[303] *Cf.* VI, pp. 6 and 7 ; VIII, p. 16.
[304] *Cf.* I, p. 11.
[305] Sir J. W. Pease makes it average for the seven years 1874-82 about 1s. 4d.,
including the exceptional case of December, 1879, when it rose to 3s. by the
advance of 12½ per cent.; *cf.* IV, p. 24. It was 1s. 7·24d. exactly between
1876-85 ; *cf.* IX, p. 4.
[306] IX, p. 9.
[307] *Cf.* III, p. 11 ; IV, p. 9 ; VI, pp. 7 and 9.
[308] *Cf.* II, p. 11 ; IV, p. 17 ; VI, p. 7.

1s. 6d. over shillings does make full allowance for the 5 per cent. value attaching to a time bargain.[300]

(v). Such then are the chief disadvantages and difficulties which seem to attach to arbitration. In the first place there is the possibility that the award may not meet with loyal adherence. In the second place, despite of the courteous attitude of either side, the formality of procedure which must to some extent be imported into these matters, and the preparation of elaborate arguments thereby entailed, are likely to engender some contentiousness, and to leave behind a little soreness. And in the third and last place, an element of possible uncertainty, and of real and serious difficulty, is introduced by the necessity of discovering some definite principle on which the award may be based, and of ascertaining with exactitude the data which are to guide the application of the principle to the particular circumstances of the moment.

It need hardly be shown in detail that these objections attach in the same manner—and in the case of the second at least in a very much more intensified degree—to "strikes" and "lock-outs," and to irregular negotiations during the continuance of these struggles. If indeed the ultimate appeal is made to force, it is evident that the party which has proved the weaker must abide for the time by the terms of capitulation, but it is only too likely to be ready to take up arms again the moment it imagines that it is stronger than its opponent. Peace is indeed secured for the time, but the feelings which prompt to war are left behind, unchanged and unchanging. Nor is either party likely to arrive at any definite principle on which the decision of the dispute can be based, save that alone of the might of the stronger, when they regard one another as enemies, to whom they are unwilling to reveal, if they can help it, the circumstances of their own position, and upon whose advances and statements they look with suspicion, reluctant to credit the former with genuineness or the latter with accuracy.

But it is with respect to the second of the disadvantages to which we have just alluded, that industrial peace, however maintained, is so signally superior to industrial warfare. There is indeed an element of contentiousness attaching to arbitration, but it is as nothing compared with that attaching to "strikes" and "lock-outs." Arbitration allows room for the growth—gradual though it may be—of amicable feelings; industrial strife stereotypes and perpetuates an attitude of implacable hostility. Many and many a failure in arbitration—disappointing as those failures may be—may yet find ample compensation in a single instance where the two disputants have agreed to refer the settlement of their quarrel to the peaceful mediation of a neutral party. It is the promise of the future which is the basis at once of the hopefulness of arbitration and the despair of industrial conflict. For when once the opposing parties have met on an equal footing, and have learnt to rely for the maintenance of their claims upon argument rather than force, they have taken the first and most difficult step upon the path which conducts naturally to conciliation—to mutual concession instead of contentious argument.

For the value of conciliation chiefly lies in this—that from its very nature it reduces the element of contentiousness to a minimum, even if it does not dispense with it altogether. And, with this element of contentiousness gone, the danger of infringement of the articles of peace, and the difficulty of arriving at a definite principle and of agreeing upon accurate data, do not indeed become inconsiderable, but do lose half, or more than half, of their seriousness. For, from the very statement of the case, it is clear that either side is likely to abide by the decision to which it has willingly agreed ; and the difficulties of the peaceful settlement of a quarrel have a happy faculty of disappearing when either side is prepared to make mutual concessions, is anxious to com to an agreement, is habituated to friendly intercourse and courteous discussion. Nor is accuracy of data more unlikely to be secured when both sides are ready to furnish evidence, and to listen to the evidence supplied by their opponents, and when the persons engaged in the discussion are *ex hypothesi* well acquainted with the technical details and industrial history of the trade.

We must not however forget that these two disadvantages do attach in a minor degree to conciliation as well as to arbitration. For there is a possibility that the constituents may not abide by the negotiations of their representatives at the board of conciliation, and there is also some difficulty in determining the proper basis for the settlement, and discovering the exact data required. And in the background at least there must be provision for reference to arbitration in some form or other, if there is to be any way out of a deadlock.

CHAPTER IV.

The Third Stage: the Establishment of Sliding Scales.

(A) Conciliation, when thoroughly established and recognised, may pave the way for what may be called the automatic regulation of wages by sliding scales. These scales have been successfully adopted in the mining industries, and especially among the colliers in some parts of England; and for a typical example of their operation we may take the coal trades of Durham and Northumberland. The principle on which they are based has been explained with some detail by Professor Munro,[310] and is briefly this: wages are to vary according to the selling price of the coal. A time is settled when the relation between wages and prices is agreed by both parties to be fair, and the scale is based upon this relation. The price paid at that time for coal is termed the "standard" price, and the wages then paid are the "standard" wages. This then is the general principle, although it admits, as we shall see, of considerable variety upon points of detail; and Professor Munro gives an exhaustive definition of a sliding scale in these terms: it is a "method by which wages, based on a " standard wage payable at a standard price, rise or fall an agreed " percentage with every agreed rise or fall in the average price of " coal at the mines, such average price being ascertained at fixed " intervals."[311]

(i). Thus, according to the first sliding scale adopted[312] in the Durham coal trade, the standard wage was to be paid when the standard price of 5s. 8d. to 6s. 4d. was realised. If the price fell between 5s. 8d. and 5s. 4d. the wages for the "underground-men" were to fall 5 per cent., and for "surface-men" 4 per cent. below the standard rate. If again the price fell lower than 5s. 4d., the wages of the "underground-men" were to fall 7½ per cent., and of "surface-men" 6 per cent. below the same point. And if, on the other hand, prices rose higher than 6s. 4d., a rise of 5 per cent.

---

[310] Cf. "Sliding Scales in the Coal Industry;" and also "Sliding Scales in the " Iron Industry."

[311] Cf. op. cit., p. 6.   [312] Cf. op. cit., p. 20.

for "underground-men " and of 4 per cent. for " surface-men "
above the standard wage was to be made for every advance of 8_d._
in prices. A minimum rate of 2_s._ 9_d._ a day for "able-bodied men
" above ground " was also fixed. Prices were to be ascertained at
the end of every March, July, and November by two accountants
sworn to secrecy—the one selected by the owners, and the other by
the men, and paid at their joint expense—and the prices thus
obtained were to be the "average net price realised for all coal
" raised at the pit's mouth during the four months " preceding the
time of investigation. The agreement was to last for two years.

But it was found that the standard relation of wages to prices
had been fixed too high for the period of depression which followed.
The arrangement for the minimum wage seems also to have
created dissatisfaction, and a strike occurred which lasted some
weeks.   Arbitration was invoked in July, 1879, to determine
whether or not a reduction should be made in the rates of wages;
and it is to be noticed at this point that a sliding scale does not
necessarily dispense with all recourse to arbitration, for under the
scale of 1877 provision had been expressly made for reference to
an umpire, and the discontinuance of the scale in 1879 compelled
a return to the old system of fixing wages in accordance with the
awards of arbitrators. In the October, however, of the same year
a fresh sliding scale was adopted, and the award of Lord Derby
was now taken as the basis. The standard price was fixed at
4_s._ 2_d._ to 4_s._ 6_d._[313] For every advance of 4_d._ in prices, there was
to be a rise of 2½ per cent. in the wages of "underground-men,"
and of enginemen, mechanics, and cokemen, and of 2 per cent. in the
wages of all other "surface-men ; " and for every fall of 4_d._ there
was to be a similar reduction of 2½ and 2 per cent. The only
exception to this uniform rate of advance and reduction was to be
made in the event of a rise in price from 5_s._ 10_d._ to 6_s._ 2_d._, when
the rate of advance in wages was to be for this stage—and for this
stage only—5 and 4 per cent. Prices were to be ascertained in the
same manner as under the previous scale ; and this second scale
was to continue in force until 31st December, 1881, and then to be
terminable on a six months' notice given by either party.

In April, 1882, a revision was once more made.[314] The standard
price was now lowered to 3_s._ 10_d._ to 4_s._ 0_d._, and the rate of advance
or reduction was fixed at 1¼ and 1 per cent. in wages for every 2_d._
in prices, the stage between 5_s._ 10_d._ and 6_s._ 2_d._ being distinguished,
as before, by a double rate of advance or reduction. In addition to
the regulations for ascertaining the prices contained in the two
previous scales, it was provided that "the quantity of all coals

313 _Cf._ _op._ _cit._, p. 22.   314 _Cf._ _op._ _cit._, p. 24.

" disposed of otherwise than for colliery purposes, be ascertained " and priced at the average selling price of coal of a similar " description, and the sum thus arrived at to be added to the " sales;" and also "that the quantities raised be checked by the " quantities sold, consumed, and stocked." The agreement was to continue in force "absolutely" until 30th June, 1883, and was thenceforward to be terminable on six months' notice from either party; and the periods of revision of prices and wages were to be reduced under the scale from four to three months.

In June, 1884, a fourth scale[315] was established on the same basis, to continue in force until 31st July, 1886, and then to be terminable on the 31st July, either of that or of any succeeding year, after a two months' previous notice had been lodged by either party.

(ii). In the Northumberland coal trade the first scale was adopted in 1879 after a period of some considerable dissension between masters and men.[316] The standard price and wage were to be those of November, 1878,[317] the former then being 5s. 1·28d., the latter 4s. 9½d. Wages were to vary 2½ per cent. in the case " of underground workmen" and "bankmen," and 2 per cent. in that of "screeners and other surface-labourers," for every variation of 4d. in price—with the exception that every rise of 1s. 4d. in price was to carry an extra-advance of 2½ and 2 per cent. in wages. The method of ascertaining the prices was similar to that employed in Durham, and "changes in wage" were to be "based " on the total sums of money received between the intervals of " each ascertainment, divided by the total quantity of coal raised " in the same time." The period of ascertainment was to be every three months, and the agreement was to last "for one year from " the date of the first ascertainment subject to a month's notice." In 1883 the scale was revised[318] and the standard price reduced to 4s. 8d. The advance, or reduction, as the case might be, was fixed at 1¼ and 1 per cent. for every 2d. in prices with an "extra 1½ per " cent. advance," at the following prices : 6s., 6s. 4d., 7s. 2d., 7s. 8d., 8s. 6d., and 9s. An arrangement was made that, unless notice was given one month previously to the 31st of December of any year of intention to terminate the agreement at that date, it should continue in force from year to year.[319]

(iii). These sliding scales admit, as we have noticed, of considerable diversity of detail. For both in Northumberland and in Durham there is frequent occasion for the action of the joint

---

[315] Cf. op. cit., p. 26.   [316] Cf. infra, p. 106.
[317] Cf. "Sliding Scales in the Coal Industry," p. 28.
[318] Cf. op. cit., p. 29.
[319] This notice was given towards the close of 1886.

committees. The standard wage indeed is the average wage of
the county, but it by no means follows that this wage is paid to
every individual miner. For, as Professor Munro states,[320] "not
"only will wages vary from colliery to colliery," but "in the
"same colliery apparent differences of wages will exist." The
nature of the seam and the difficulty of working it are taken
into account; and indeed it would appear that some other elements
as well enter into the matter, "for the different rates per seam"
supplied in a table printed in Professor Munro's pamphlet "do
"not result in an equal daily wage." "The real standard
"wages" then "for any particular colliery," in Northumberland
for instance, are the wages paid at that colliery to the different
classes of labourers in November, 1878. For the prices and wages
then paid were taken as the starting point of the first scale in
the Northumberland coal trade.

And so side by side with the sliding scales in Northumberland
and Durham we find the action of the joint committees. The
average wage for the county fluctuates in accordance with fluctuations in prices in the manner arranged by the scale, and the
particular wages at particular collieries fluctuate also in accordance
with the fluctuations in county prices; but in addition to this the
joint committee may be called upon from time to time to effect
local and special readjustments. We have before alluded[321] to the
action of these committees, but the matter will perhaps be placed
in a clearer light by two illustrative instances. Thus we read in
a local newspaper[322] that at two collieries the "hewers" had
received notice from the head manager of a "local reduction in the
"hewing prices." At one of these collieries 2d. per ton was
demanded off the prices for the yard seam, and 2d. per ton off the
Low Main, *exclusive* of the last 1¼ per cent. reduction effected by
the county sliding scale. The men held a meeting to discuss the
matter, and then offered 1½d. reduction on the "pillar" working of
the Low Main, and 2d. a ton on the yard seam including the last
1¼ per cent. by the county sliding scale. The offer was refused,
and another meeting was held. At this the men passed a resolution stating that they had made a fair offer, and that, should it be
again refused, the case should be submitted to the joint committee.
At the other colliery, where the masters wanted a reduction of
4½d. a ton off the Telford way in the yard seam, a compromise was
effected, and a reduction of 4d. per ton on the "loose end" places,
and 2d. on the places "going in the fast" was arranged. Another

[320] *Cf. op. cit.*, p. 16.
[321] *Cf. supra*, p. 38.
[322] "Newcastle Daily Chronicle," 1st February, 1886.

paper contains[323] a reference to a dispute at a colliery where the men decided by 75 votes to 39 to send in a fortnight's notice in order to obtain an alteration in the standard of wages. A deputation waited upon the executive of the Northumberland Miners' Union, and was informed that, by the rules of the union, a majority of two-thirds was requisite before the declaration of a strike, and, as this had not been obtained, the notices could not be issued. These two instances, about the first of which there is nothing of an unusual character, may serve to exemplify the necessity and the operation of the joint committees in the coal trades of Northumberland and Durham.

B (i). The chief advantages of these sliding scales may be said to lie on the one hand in their elasticity, and on the other in their automatic action. For, as we shall see hereafter, and as the diversity of local application which characterises the scales in the Durham and Northumberland coal trades so strikingly illustrates, they admit of adaptation—to an extent which has entered as yet, perhaps not even into the conception, and certainly not into the practice, of those actually engaged in industry—to the most diversified situations. Nor is it necessary to prove the obvious fact that during the time these scales continue in operation the general fluctuations of wages proceed with automatic precision, and therefore the possibility of general friction is inconsiderable. And, as a consequence of this automatic regularity, it follows, as Professor Munro has stated,[324] that sliding scales "give a "steadiness" on the one hand to trade, and on the other to wages.

It is hardly necessary to say that the recurrence of industrial disputes promotes instability in trade. It may indeed be argued that, when a strike follows a period of over production in some branch of industry, it may result in clearing the market more thoroughly than would otherwise be done.[325] It may also be the case that conditions have been inserted in contracts providing for the special contingency of a strike. But the fact still remains that employers are likely to prosecute their industrial undertakings with greater confidence; to avail themselves of fresh openings with more vigorous enterprise; and to make a fuller use of existing opportunities, if they are freed from all reasonable apprehension of a sudden and forcible cessation of industry. The mere rumour of a strike must

---

[323] *Cf.* "Newcastle Daily Leader," 9th March, 1886. Mr. R. Young informs me that in this case reference was not made to the joint committee because the colliery owners did *not* belong to the Masters' Association, and therefore could *not* appeal to the committee. In other cases the decision of *all* disputes rests with the committee, on appeal being made by either party.

[324] *Cf.* "Sliding Scales in the Coal Industry," pp. 17 and 18.

[325] *Cf.* "The Wages Question," by F. A. Walker, p. 391, foot note; also Report of Royal Commission on Depression of Trade. Q. 5267—9 and 5760.

exercise an appreciable influence upon the bold conduct of commerce;
its actual occurrence is only too often an incontestable calamity.
And even under the more peaceful system of arbitration some
friction is likely, and some delay is occasioned, in the settlement of
a dispute; and the least amount of friction, and the shortest
period of delay, must exercise—though indeed in a less degree
than a strike—a prejudicial influence upon commercial enterprise.
Nor again if the trade is one of great fluctuation can an arbitrator
fairly fix wages for a very long period, for he cannot foresee the
changes in prices which are likely to occur.[326] But a sliding scale,
on the other hand, as Mr. Watson argues,[327] " is the simplest and
" therefore the best method. It does not settle trade disputes, it
" avoids them."[328]

In the manufactured iron trade, where indeed scales have been
introduced on four different occasions—in 1872, in 1874, in 1880,
and in 1883—and have then been abandoned, we find the employers
insisting upon their advantages before different arbitrators. " We
" thought," remarks[329] one of their number before Mr. Dale in
1877, that a sliding scale " would avoid all kinds of contention,
" and all kinds of dispute with regard to the *equilibrium* between
" selling price on the one hand and the rate of wages on the
" other." " It was a great support to me to have such a thing as a
" sliding scale, and an Arbitration Board like this to step in to seize
" hold of my difficulties, and cut them as it were in a moment,"
" without any trouble or any anxiety of my own." " I believe our
" umpire and every employer here would be only too delighted if
" we could get some standard or scale."[330] And similarly before
Sir Joseph Pease in 1882 they urge[331] that the " system of sliding
" scales has its special advantages. It is exact and systematic."
" It has enabled the employers of the north to provide regular
" work for their men, and the development of the Northern Iron
" trade has been the result of the system." Before Mr. Watson,
again, in 1884, the president[332] alludes to the " advantages " which
the sliding scale " gives to the employers in making their contracts,
" and insuring regular work;" and, as we have before noticed,[333] a
controversy arose between them and the men in 1885, upon the very
question whether the 5 per cent., which was the admitted *value* of a
time-bargain, *and therefore of a sliding scale arrangement*, was, or
was not, included in the 1s. 6d. above shillings for pounds allowed
in the scales of 1880 and 1883. The men on their part, although

[326] *Cf.* I. p. 4 ; V, p. 4.   [327] *Cf.* " Boards of Arbitration," p. 17.
[328] *Cf.* Report of Royal Commission on Depression of Trade. Q. 11713—6,
12341, 1243b—45.
[329] *Cf.* I, p. 8.   [330] *Cf.* I, p. 17.   [331] *Cf.* IV, p. 10.
[332] *Cf.* VI, p. 9.   [333] *Cf.* supra, p. 70.

disapproving of these two scales, and declining to attribute the success of the board to any system of sliding scales,[334] recognise the value of the system on more than one occasion. "If we "can agree," Mr. Trow, for instance, says before Mr. Dale in 1879,[335] "on some sliding scale to regulate our wages, it will be "much to the benefit of the trade and save much unpleasantness, "as we shall know exactly at the end of each quarter what we "shall have to receive the next quarter."

The arbitrator himself, Mr. Dale, is reported[336] to have once observed of the sliding scale system, that it was not "alternative "to, or competitive with, that of conciliation or arbitration." "It "is," he added, "an outcome and development of conciliation, and "its base may be made, and indeed has been made, the subject of "arbitration." "The sliding-scale plan can be justified both on "theoretical and practical grounds," and, when based upon the independent examination of the employers' books, "it secures for "the operative class a knowledge absolutely unobtainable other- "wise of the relative condition of trade at all times." Sir Joseph Pease,[337] again, in his award of November, 1882, sums up the benefits of a sliding scale in these terms. "It gives," he argues, "to the capitalist an undoubted advantage in his competition in "the markets of the world, which is also of essential service to the "operative; whilst it secures to the operative that increased pay "for his labour, which naturally follows the increased demand for, "and consequent profit upon, the article which his labour pro- "duces; and in times of depression its tendency must be to enable "the capitalist to keep his works going, and his hands employed "until brighter times dawn again upon them." And Mr. Watson, in his award of December, 1884, strongly urges[338] the establishment of a fresh scale, because, he maintains, "the automatic action of "a sliding scale prevents even the slight collision entailed by the "negotiations consequent upon conciliation."

(ii). But not only does a sliding scale thus tend to promote stability in trade, but it also, as a necessary consequence of this, tends to promote stability in wages. This latter point indeed may not appear to be so obvious as the former. For at first sight the tendency of a scale may seem to be the very reverse of this. If wages are to fluctuate with variations in price, then it may seem that they will be continuously moving up and down, and that instability rather than steadiness will be the result. But, before we accept this conclusion, there are several considerations to be borne in mind. For under a system of periodical arbitration there

[334] Cf. IV, p. 15.   [335] Cf. III, p. 14.
[336] Cf. VI, p. 9.   [337] Cf. V, pp. 4, 11; IV, pp. 3. 23.
[338] Cf. VIII, p. 17; VI, p. 20.

may be a similar fluctuation in wages. Owing to the changes in prices there may be repeated recourse to arbitration. In the Durham coal trade immediately before the institution of the first sliding scale there were nine successive arbitrations within the space of two years; and in the manufactured iron trade the workmen complain[339] before Mr. Watson in November, 1884, that the constant resort that had been made to arbitration within the past year was calculated to undermine the very existence of the board, and was in an eminent degree an "anti-conciliatory" policy. Nor, as a matter of fact, do most sliding scales contemplate any continual fluctuation in wages. In the coal trade the Somerset scale is an exception—and apparently a solitary exception—in providing that every rise or fall in prices shall be accompanied by a rise or fall in wages. In most cases prices are to be ascertained only at definite intervals—sometimes every six months, as in the South Wales' Association scale of 1875; sometimes every four months, as in the first two Durham scales and in the South Wales' scales of 1880 and 1882; sometimes, again, every three months, as in the last two Durham scales, the Northumberland, the Cumberland, the Ocean, and the Ferndale scales; sometimes every month, as in the Bedworth scale.[340]   Of course it may happen that the period of readjustment fixed by the scale may prove to be too long; and in the manufactured iron trade, where the prices under the scales of 1871, 1874, and 1880, were ascertained every three months, the last scale seems to have excited dissatisfaction and to have been abandoned, partly[341] at least, because it was too slow in its action and was not speedy enough in giving the men the benefit of a rise in prices, or in securing a reduction of wages when prices were falling. At any rate the accountant's returns, which continue to be made in the north of England—but not in Staffordshire[342]—when a scale is not in operation, were furnished, under the Durham scale of 1883, every two months,[343] and this practice has since been followed. But, even if the periods when prices are ascertained are comparatively frequent, yet some definite interval at least is taken, and there is no fluctuation of wage from week to week. Nor again do wages vary with every fluctuation of price, but only with those of a certain amount. The sliding scale, once more, is, to some extent, no inadequate guarantee for regular employment. For there is little fear of the interruption caused by a strike or lock-out; and the very stability thus ensured to the conduct of

339 *Cf.* VIII, p. 4.
340 *Cf.* "Sliding Scales in the Coal Industry," pp. 20—52.
341 *Cf.* IV, p. 6; V, p. 4.
342 *Cf.* VIII, p. 8.
343 *Cf.* VI, pp. 7 and 9; VII, p. 6.

trade encourages the enterprise and confidence of employers, and tends to make the trade itself and the workers more prosperous.

The importance of this stability of wage and regularity of employment can hardly be over-estimated. Mr. Mawdsley is but expressing the truth when he writes,[344] the fluctuation of wages is the "bane of our class;" and Professor Marshall calls attention[345] to another aspect of the same truth when he states, "forced interruption to labour is a terrible evil." For a constant alternation between high and low wages unsettles the character and the habits of a man; and irregularity of employment affects in a similar way his physical, his mental, his moral aptitude for work. The habits of expenditure formed in a time of extravagant prosperity may lead in a time of sudden adversity to debt, of the burden of which it may take a lifetime to effect a riddance; and a period of leisure, which would recruit the exhausted energies of a man if it came at regular intervals, will of itself be likely to undermine his strength and efficiency for work if it occurs at irregular periods, or amid the pressure of pecuniary embarrassments. Far "better" were it "for a family," argues Mr. Mawdsley,[346] "to have 35s. per week for fifty weeks in the year, than 40s. for "twenty-five, and 31s. per week for the other twenty-five;" and better too, we may add, is it likely to be for employers and for the nation as a whole, if the efficiency of labour be taken into account, as it must be on any sound theory of production or distribution. The coal and iron industries are liable to considerable fluctuations, because they necessarily suffer when other industries are depressed—and in the Northumberland coal trade, at least, the trade seems to have been periodically slack in the winter when the Baltic is closed—but, if men and masters can look forward for a period of three or more months to definite certainty in industrial relations, this element of fluctuation loses half its injurious effects, and the condition of things is yet further improved when changes in wages only follow upon changes of a certain amount in prices.

iii (a). A further question of no little interest suggests itself with regard to the future consequences of sliding scales. Do they or do they not tend in the direction of industrial partnership? Jevons maintains[347] that "both the sliding scale and the system "of arbitration generally" ought to be regarded as a "stepping "stone to some still sounder method of partnership and participa- "tion in profits which a future generation will certainly enjoy."

---

[344] *Cf.* I. R. C. Report, p. 158.   [345] *Cf. op. cit.*, p. 175.
[346] *Cf. op. cit.*, p. 158.
[347] *Cf.* "State in Relation to Labour," p. 158.

Mr. Watson says[348] that the sliding scale "is no doubt a distinct "step in the direction of industrial co-partnership." But we cannot help thinking that this conclusion requires to be stated with some modification; for the evidence upon the point appears to tell in a negative as well as an affirmative direction.

In the first place, the successful conduct of conciliation or arbitration, and the continued operation of sliding scales, depend in a very large degree upon the strength of the organisations of men and masters on either side. It is indeed true that the first board of conciliation in the manufactured iron trade of Staffordshire seems to have failed because it was confined to the local branch of the Ironworkers' Union, and those ironworkers who were outside the ranks of the union did not consider themselves bound by the decisions of the board;[349] but this fact tends rather to show the necessity of an union strong enough to secure the actual allegiance of at least the great majority of the men, and the probable concurrence of the non-unionist minority. It is true again that in the iron trade of the north of England we find the representative of the men contending[350] before Mr. Watson in 1884 that both masters and men ought to "forget" their respective associations at the meetings of the board, and that "the Board "should be able to decide all questions submitted to it without "the interference of any other association;" and this contention seems to be reasonable. But on the other hand there appears to be equal reason in the argument of the representative of the employers,[351] that the board is "founded upon the idea of organisa-"tions on both sides;" and before Mr. Dale in 1877 the men themselves allude[352] to the possible difficulty which might be experienced in securing the adherence of the "strong non-union "element" to the award of the arbitrator. It is indeed sufficiently obvious that the decisions of courts of arbitration and the arrangements of a sliding scale will be of little avail unless masters and men are willing to abide by them. This they are not likely to do unless the negotiators are thoroughly representative; and this thorough representation can hardly be secured save through the medium of an association of masters on the one side and of men on the other. Sir Rupert Kettle once stated[353] that he confessed that he saw "no organisation but" that of "trades unions" upon which to fall back "for the purpose of conducting the business" of these boards and of electing workmen's delegates; and the reply[354] of

[348] Cf. "Boards of Arbitration," &c., p. 17.
[349] Cf. "Industrial Conciliation," p. 64.   [350] Cf. VIII, p. 7.
[351] Cf. VIII, p. 10.   [352] Cf. I, p. 14.
[353] Cf. Report, by J. D. Weeks, sec. xi, p. 26.
[354] Cf. Second Report, part i, Appendix B, p. 400, ans. 14 (a).

the Newcastle Chamber of Commerce to the questions addressed
to it by the Royal Commission on the Depression of Trade very
aptly illustrates this point. "Very little change," it writes, "has
" taken place recently in the relations between capital and labour,
" except that they have become steadier, chiefly through the work-
" men's trade unions being well organised, and being met by like
" organisations of employers; circumstances which, in some cases,
" have led to the formation of boards of conciliation and the
" regulation of wages by the market values of the productions."

But if, on the one hand, the existence of strong associations
on either side appears in this way to be necessary, if "increased
"organisation" really "means decreased war," it is, on the other
hand, obvious that the idea which lies at the bottom of trades
unionism is the antagonism of interests between masters and men;
and hence it might seem that a system which rests upon trades
unionism, whether of masters or of men, as its basis, is scarcely
calculated to result in a system which is the very opposite of trades
unionism. Masters and men may indeed meet round a common
table and arrive at a common agreement; but they meet as representatives of associations which have been formed on either side for
the avowed purpose of protection against the other side, and they
arrive at an agreement on the negative ground of the injury and
irritation caused by a strike, rather than on the positive basis of
an acknowledged identity of interests. It is a great point gained
that they should meet and that they should agree; and a sense of
identity of interests may be the ultimate outcome of this.

But even then it seems likely that, so far at least as the action of
the sliding scale itself is concerned, this identity will be an identity
not between the employer and employed of a certain business
undertaking, but rather between a combination of employers and
a combination of employed. There is apparently no necessary
tendency in such an arrangement to transpose industrial divisions
from the "horizontal" to the "perpendicular"—to use Jevons's
expressive illustration[355]—from the opposition of workmen as a
body to employers as a body, to the opposition of the workers,
employer and employed alike, in a single undertaking to the
workers in another undertaking. There are indeed grounds for
supposing that the tendency is in the opposite direction; for to
some extent at least the respective capacity of men and masters
does not result in direct advantage to themselves, but affects the
condition of those engaged in the trade as a whole. Payment by
piece, indeed, which is the general practice in the coal and iron
trades, has, as Professor Marshall has pointed out,[356] an element of

[355] *Cf.* "State in Relation to Labour," p. 145.
[356] *Cf.* "Economics of Industry," III, IX, sec. ii.

co-operation in its nature, for both employers and employed are
directly interested in an additional output. But, so far as this
argument has weight, the payment by piece is merely part of the
mechanism adopted by particular sliding scales, and is scarcely to
be regarded as belonging to the essence of the system. It is of
course true, over and beyond the results of payment by piece, that
the output is likely to be greater when prices are higher, and
consequently by the arrangement of the scale wages also are
higher; and that therefore employers and employed have a
coincident interest in an increased output on account of increased
prices. But this identity of interest is so far only probable and
contingent, and belongs to them rather as a body than to those
connected with a particular mine. It is obvious also that the
workmen of a particular mine benefit in the way of regularity of
employment if their employer exhibits more capacity than his
fellows, and can thereby secure a larger amount of business. But
on the other hand the method of ascertaining the average price is
likely, in the probable contingency that a particular employer is
enabled by his superior business capacity to obtain a greater
number of orders and sales at higher prices than his competitors
in the trade, to distribute part of the benefits of this over the
whole body of the workmen affected by the scale, and to subject
his fellow employers to a corresponding disadvantage. For the
net average price has been ascertained, in the case of the coal
mining scales, by the inspection of the books of all the owners; and
in the case of the iron industries by a similar examination of the
books—in some instances of all, in others of a selected number—
of the firms. The net selling prices thus ascertained are added
together to form one sum; this sum is divided by the total quantities of the commodities sold, and the result of this division is
taken as the average price of the scale. It is on the variations in
this average that fluctuations in the average wage, and the local
modifications of that, are based. But it is obvious that the extensive sale of the coal of a particular colliery at a high price would
result in an increase in the average price, and would thus occasion
a rise of wages not only to the miners at the particular colliery,
the owner of which had by his business capacity, or from any
other cause, secured this sale, but also to the whole body of miners
affected by the scale. And a corresponding expense in wages would
be entailed not merely upon the particular owner who had secured
the high price, but also upon the other owners who had only
realised a lower price. And so there would be nothing in this to
separate the interests of the men in the particular colliery from
those of the general body, and to associate them closely with those
of their own individual employer; but it would be far more likely

that the general body of the men, finding that their wages were rising as a whole—setting aside variations of a local character—would so far regard their interests as essentially common.

Similar conclusions may also be based upon cases like that of the Northumberland coal trade, where there is a broad division between the "steam-coal" and the "soft-coal" collieries. Before Lord Herschell in 1875 an owner stated[357] that "it would be found "in investigating the accounts of any one particular colliery," that "there would be a very great difference in the prices obtained for "the different classes of coal." "At one colliery," he added, "it "would be one price, and at another colliery it would be another "price, and so on." In order therefore to avoid complication, the gross sales and the gross prices had been taken by the owners as the basis on which the average net selling price was to be calculated. This statement was made in answer to an objection raised by the men, and allowed by the umpire, on the ground that the sales of coal at the "steam-coal" collieries had not been distinguished from those at the "soft-coal" collieries in the accounts supplied by the owners; and that therefore by averaging the two the workmen in the one branch of the trade which was prospering might "suffer" because the other branch was not in a prosperous state. In the same way it appeared in argument before Sir Lyon Playfair that the sale of the small coal was a very variable element, sometimes commanding a market and sometimes not; and his award was based in the main upon this consideration.[358] At some collieries also it seems that some other commodity, such as clay or bricks, is produced in addition to coal, and this, the owners allege, does enter as an item into the calculations of selling prices.[359] In Durham again there are four great classes of coal—gas coal, manufacturing coal, household coal, and coking coal;[360] but these classes do not appear to be distinguished in the accountants' returns. In all these cases then the men are treated as a whole, although it is manifest that an increased sale of the coal which realises one price, and a diminished sale of that which realises another, would affect the average price. But, despite of this, it is as a whole that the men are treated, so far as the alteration in the average wage, on which the local variations are indirectly based, is concerned; although the average price, on which the average wage itself is based, is influenced by circumstances peculiar, it may be, to the men of a particular class of colliery—perhaps even to the men of a single colliery.

This point is emphasised by the reports of the proceedings

---

[357] Cf. H, pp. 37 and 39.
[358] Cf. P, pp. 133 and 134, and supra, p. 59.
[359] Cf. H, pp. 61 and 63.   [360] Cf. H, p. 109.

at courts of arbitration in the manufactured iron trade. For the masters urge[361] before Mr. Dale in 1877 that in the face of the sudden decline—or indeed the practical disappearance—of the iron rail trade, it would be fair to rest their claim for a reduction upon a comparison of the prices of plates, bars, and angles alone; and before Mr. Shaw-Lefevre in 1878 they do, as a matter of fact, omit[362] the prices of rails from the statement they place before the arbitrator. The men on their part contend[363] before Mr. Dale in 1879, that the evidence furnished by a comparison of the past and present returns of the accountant must be discounted by the consideration that in the averages of past years the prices realised by certain firms which manufactured higher-priced classes of iron had been included, but were now excluded; and that the appeal to the so-called " Thorneycroft basis," to which the employers had referred, was similarly vitiated on the ground that it had been based not upon the prices realised by all the firms concerned, but only upon those secured by a few leading firms. Before Mr. Watson again they maintain[364] that the prices quoted by the employers from the " Iron and Coal Trades Review" are misleading, because they are based on those of the very lowest-priced classes of iron, and their wages, according to traditional custom, are determined by the average obtained by adding together into one sum the prices of all classes and every quality.

The point we have noticed may of course be said to be in some sense of an accidental nature, and by no means to attach of necessity to sliding scales; and this is true so far as the different classes of iron and coal enter into the matter. It might indeed be difficult in practice to effect a separation between the different classes and qualities of the articles produced, if that separation were not confined to the broadest differences, but were carried down to the minute and manifold distinctions of quality which are to be found in almost any industry. But the separation, it must be admitted, turns upon the question of introducing fresh complications into the calculations of the accountants, and of incurring additional expense.[365] It seems, from a theoretical standpoint, to be possible, and the result we have just been considering appears to be in some measure the consequence of including in one combination of employers or employed men whose circumstances are essentially different. For by acting as a whole they must of necessity waive individual distinctions so far as the average price is concerned. But the way in which the average price is affected by the individual enterprise of

---

[361] *Cf.* I, p. 5.   [362] *Cf.* II, p. 3.
[363] *Cf.* III, p. 10.   [364] *Cf.* VII, p. 4.
[365] *Cf.* " Sliding Scales in the Coal Industry," pp. 35, 37 and 38; and *contra*, p. 41.

a particular employer is a factor which cannot be eliminated; and on this ground, if on no other, it seems that a sliding scale does not necessarily tend in the direction of industrial partnership.

The point, however, is a nice one in theory, and its exact influence in practice may not be very important. But it derives support from other considerations of a similar purport and a more obvious character. For a sliding scale, it must be remembered, does not proceed upon any avowed theory of sharing in profits, but only upon a theory of participation in prices. The amount of profits indeed is jealously kept from the knowledge of the public, the workmen and rival employers;[366] and the accountants, who investigate the books and compile the returns, are sworn to secrecy. The employers stoutly maintain[367] that the wages of the men have nothing to do with profits; and the consideration of "costs of "production" is excluded from the arrangement of the scales. The attitude thus adopted is scarcely calculated to lead to an avowed industrial partnership.

One other point deserves a passing notice. Under a system of industrial partnership the share allowed out of profits would be paid on profits actually secured; in a sliding scale the rate of wages paid for the quarter, or the four months as the case may be, is based upon the selling prices of the previous period, which may not indeed be actually realised during the succeeding period; and hence the reason for the greater frequency with which prices have been ascertained in the manufactured iron trade under the Durham arrangement of 1883.

(b). But although these considerations must discount to some extent the probability of the development of a system of industrial partnership out of a system of sliding scales, there are also opposing considerations which must not be forgotten.

In the first place, although the system of sliding scales is generally based upon hostile combinations, and recognises as a necessary factor the outward form of trades unionism, and therefore in some degree intensifies the latent spirit of opposition which must underlie, in some measure at least, that outward form, yet the mere fact that the two combinations meet and effect a mutual arrangement, is a distinct step towards abolishing the open feud and mitigating the hostile spirit. Nor should it be forgotten that profit-sharing, as it has been hitherto practised in England, has refused in most cases to recognise the position of trades unions,

---

[366] Cf. for unwillingness of English employers to disclose profits, "Report of "Royal Commission upon Depression of Trade," Q. 12, 13, and 4022. Under the Ocean Scale even the average price is kept secret, and the rate of wages due by the scale is alone made known. Cf. "Sliding Scales in the Coal Industry," p. 45.

[367] Cf. K, p. 9.

and to extend its advantages to those who still adhere to an
association, and that therefore the reconciliation of trades unionism
with industrial partnership has scarcely as yet been subjected to a
fair or decisive test.

In the second place, the sliding scale is based upon an identity
of interests between employers and employed, so far as price is
concerned. The object of both sides is to secure the highest price
they can. "I have always considered," said Sir Rupert Kettle,[368]
sitting as arbitrator in the Northumberland coal trade, "that the
" interests of the employer and the workmen were identical until
" price was secured ;" and this identity is expressly recognised by
the very construction of a sliding scale. So far there is a quasi-
partnership. The profits of the employer are likely to be increased
if prices rise—though this may indeed be outweighed by an
increased cost of materials or machinery—and according to the
sliding scale wages are also to follow the advance in prices. Here
then we may be said to have a species of profit-sharing, for we
have a sharing in the increased profits consequent upon higher
prices ; and there is also, it may be noticed, a similar share in losses
if prices fall. Both parties have then an interest in the prosperity
and adversity of the trade. There is indeed no sharing in losses
beyond such as result under this system, as under the ordinary
system of wages, in irregularity of employment, or such as follow
peculiarly under this system as the consequence of lowered prices.
But under a regular system of profit-sharing, as it is generally
practised, the only share in losses would be of a similar nature.[369]

In the third and last place, the difficulty of making known the
details of management to the workmen—an argument which is
often advanced against a system of profit-sharing—seems to be
met, to some extent at least, by the method adopted under the
sliding scale, according to which accountants, appointed by either
side, and sworn to secrecy, examine the books of the different
firms. The chief obstacle then which remains, and which the
system of sliding scales apparently tends almost as much to
establish as to remove, is the divergence of interests between
individual masters and the particular men in their employment.
It breaks down indeed the divergence between masters and men as
a body ; but it seems to be calculated to intensify the corporate
feeling on either side, and to hinder the growth of a sense of
identity of interests between individual employers and individual
bodies of workmen. From this point of view, we may fairly
argue, there is no little truth in M. Leroy-Beaulieu's contention[370]

[368] *Cf.* K, p. 36.   [369] *Cf.* " Profit Sharing," by Sedley Taylor, p. 66.
[370] *Cf.* " Essai sur la répartition des richesses," par P. Leroy-Beaulieu,
deuxième édit., p. 374.

that it is an error of classification to place the sliding scale ("le
" salaire mobile") under the generic head of industrial partnership.

c (i). The difficulties attaching to sliding scales are similar in
their general characteristics to those with which we found that
arbitration was concerned. These were the possibility that the
decision might fail to secure loyal adherence, the contentiousness
connected with the preparation and discussion of elaborate arguments, and the difficulty of determining upon a satisfactory basis
and of ascertaining accurate data. Of these three difficulties the
second is reduced to a minimum under any system of conciliation,
and therefore amongst these under a sliding scale. But it may be
necessary to have recourse to arbitration to determine the basis of
the scale; and in the iron trade the question whether the basis of
the scale for 1880 should be 1s. 3d. or 1s. 6d. over shillings for
pounds was referred for decision to Mr. Dale, and the latter figure[371]
awarded. Even when the scale is actually in operation there may
be occasion for arbitration in the case of local disputes; and it
may be thought desirable by the one party or the other that the
basis of the scale should be altered to suit unexpected changes in
the nature of the trade. In these cases then negotiation and
arbitration, and the contentiousness connected therewith, may be
found in conjunction with a system of sliding scales. The third
difficulty also is present. There is little question indeed about
obtaining accurate data, for the books of the employers are readily
opened to the inspection of the accountants, and this point will be
sufficiently illustrated by the following extract from a local
newspaper:—[372]

" Yesterday the certificate of the accountants showing the price
" of Cleveland pig iron was issued at Middlesbrough. Under the
" sliding scale the certificate will reduce the wages of Cleveland
" miners one-half per cent. The certificate is as follows:—

" *Middlesbrough, 5th April*, 1886.

" To the Cleveland Mine Owners' Association, the Cleveland Miners' Association,
and the North-Eastern Railway Company.

" Gentlemen.—In accordance with the provisions of a memorandum of agreement, dated 10th day of July, 1885, made between the Cleveland Mine Owners'
Association of the one part, and the Cleveland Miners' Association of the other
part, for the establishment of a sliding scale, to regulate the wages of all classes of
men represented by the Cleveland Miners' Association, We the undersigned, having
obtained and verified returns from all the firms specified in the said agreement, do
hereby certify that the net average invoice price of No. 3 Cleveland pig iron for

---

[371] *Cf.* VI, p. 4.
[372] *Cf.* " Newcastle Daily Chronicle," 6th April, 1886.

the three months of January, February, and March, 1886, ascertained in the manner prescribed by the said agreement, was 31s. 9·6–5d. per ton.

" We are, Gentlemen, your obedient servants,

" MONKHOUSE, GODDARD, AND CO.,
" *Chartered Accountants, on behalf of the Cleveland Mine Owners' Association.*
" JOHN G. BENSON,
" *Chartered Accountant, on behalf of the Cleveland Miners' Association.*
" R. MACKAY AND CO.,
" *Chartered Accountants, on behalf of the North-Eastern Railway Company.*"

ii. (*a*). But there is considerable difficulty in fixing upon a basis. There must in the first instance be an agreement with regard to the general character of the basis. In most cases the selling prices are adopted by common consent as the suitable basis, and the variations in wages are to follow the fluctuations in prices. In the Northumberland coal trade this basis was generally recognised by masters and men in the arbitration proceedings to which we have referred—although other considerations were, it is true, introduced—and therefore it was to be expected that it should be readily adopted in their sliding scales. The same course has been followed in most of the scales throughout the country. In the scale which once existed in Shropshire, but was afterwards abandoned, the selling price of pig iron, and not that of coal, was taken as the basis, because the chief use to which the coal was put was the smelting of iron.[373] In the Cleveland scales again[374]—one of which regulated the wages of the ironstone miners, and the other those of the blast-furnace men, and the second of which seems to have been recently abandoned—the selling price not of the ironstone but of the manufactured product, the pig iron, and that too of a special quality, No. 3,[375] has been adopted as the basis. But it is not always easy to secure agreement to the principle that the selling prices should be the basis of the scale. In the arguments before the arbitrators in the manufactured iron trade there is, as we have seen,[376] a general understanding running throughout the cases and pleadings, both of masters and men, that wages should follow the selling prices of iron. But other considerations are again and again advanced, and the appeal to prices is by no means uniformly accepted. Sliding scales have been adopted on four

---

[373] *Cf.* " Sliding Scales in the Coal Industry," p. 55.
[374] *Cf.* " Sliding Scales in the Iron Industry," pp. 5, 6, and 8. VII, p. 6.
[375] This is done because " it has been found that practically the price of No. 3 " usually approximates to the average price of all the numbers combined.— " Sliding Scales in the Iron Industry," p. 6.
[376] *Cf. supra,* p. 62.

occasions, and have been based upon the selling prices of iron; and on four occasions they have been abandoned.

The scale which commenced in 1872 was the result of common and unanimous agreement, and was "drafted and submitted" by Mr. Dale, in consequence, as the men urge[377] before Mr. Watson in 1884, of dissatisfaction with the award of an advance of 5 per cent. given by Mr. Hughes in July, 1871. But, before it had been in working for a year, it was abandoned, because the Staffordshire ironworkers obtained an advance of 20 per cent. while the selling prices in the north only warranted an advance of $7\frac{1}{2}$ per cent. Thus the wages of the Staffordshire men were higher than those in the north to the extent of 1s. 3d.[378] The north of England men appealed, as we have previously noticed, to a principle often pleaded before arbitrators[379]—and adopted, according to the men, explicitly by Mr. Shaw-Lefevre in 1879, and implicitly by Mr. Dale in April, 1878,[380] as the basis of their awards—the principle that their wages should be on an equality with the Staffordshire rates. The masters agreed to the demand, the desired advance of $12\frac{1}{2}$ per cent. was given, and the scale suspended.

In 1874 the second scale, known as the "Derby scale," was adopted, and in this the principle of the equalisation of rates between Staffordshire and the north was openly acknowledged. For the arrangement emanated from a joint committee of employers and employed of the north and of Staffordshire. The net selling price[381] was to be ascertained by the inspection of the books of all the firms in the north, and of twelve selected firms of Staffordshire. The average selling prices of the two were to be added together, and then to be divided by two; and the result of this process was to be the average price recognised by the scale. The standard wage adopted under this scale was considerably lower than that of Mr. Dale's scale of 1871, for it was reduced from the 2s. 9d. above shillings for pounds of the 1871 scale to 9d. above shillings. The men urge[382] that this change was effected because the employers availed themselves of the congested state of the labour market, and that it was in this way also that they were enabled to enforce a reduction of 10 per cent. by mutual arrangement at York before the scale itself came into operation. The employers, however, maintain that the cost of materials, which they had pleaded before Sir Rupert Kettle at Saltburn and at Durham in 1873, and at the meeting at Birmingham in the December of the same year, compelled them to insist on this alteration.[383] The special circumstances

---

[377] Cf. VI, p. 4. [378] Cf. IV, p. 7.
[379] Cf. VI, p. 6; IX, p. 5, and supra, p. 64. [380] Cf. VI, p. 5.
[381] Cf. VI, p. 4; I, p. 11. [382] Cf. VI, p. 4; IV, p. 8.
[383] Cf. IV, p. 9.

under which the scale of 1871 had been arranged were no longer
in existence, and the revival of the basis of that scale would have
been an anachronism. This scale was in its turn abandoned—and
this time the masters seem to have been the dissatisfied parties—
before it had been more than a year in operation, and a reduction
of 5 per cent. was effected by mutual arrangement at Darlington in
July, 1875. For this course of policy the masters plead the altering
circumstances of the trade,—the general depression experienced,
and the decline of the demand for rails in particular.[384] But the
men affirm[385] that the same reason is to be given for its abandonment as that which they supplied for its basis, and that this was
the overcrowded condition of the labour market.

Five years afterwards, in 1880, a fresh scale was established
and Mr. Dale, who was asked to decide whether the basis should
be 1s. 3d. over shillings for pounds or 1s. 6d., awarded the latter
figure.[386] The scale lasted for nearly two years, but a strike took
place at the beginning of 1882 in consequence of dissatisfaction
with the figures stated in the returns of the accountant. The men
contended[387] that the conditions of the labour market were now in
their favour, and that the scale did not give them the benefit of
this; that the basis was unfair, and had been fixed by Mr. Dale at
a lower figure than he would have awarded had he possessed a "free
" hand;" and that the scale had been accepted in 1879 because it
had been accompanied by the tempting condition of an immediate
advance of 12½ per cent. The president of the board maintains, on
the other hand, that the scale did not act with sufficient celerity, as
the wages were paid in accordance with the prices realised during
the three previous months, and the prices rose with such rapidity
that those realised during the succeeding three months seemed
to be out of proportion to the wages then paid.[388] The scale was
at any rate abandoned, and an advance of 7½ per cent. given.

For the last three months of 1883 this scale was revived under
a mutual arrangement called the "Durham agreement," and this
time the prices were to be ascertained every two instead of every
three months.[389] But to this agreement, the men state,[390] they only
consented because a second condition was attached providing for
the suspension of Monday work, and a concession was added of the
continuance of the existing rates for six months—a concession
which was tantamount to the payment of 5 per cent. above the
wages allowed by the scale. The employers, on the contrary,
contend[391] that the "Durham agreement" was "confirmed and

[384] Cf. I, p. 11; IV, p. 9.
[385] Cf. IV, p. 8.   [386] Cf. VI, p. 2.
[387] Cf. IV, p. 11; VI, p. 5.   [388] Cf. IV, p. 6.
[389] Cf. VI, pp. 4, 9.   [390] Cf. VI, p. 13.   [391] Cf. VI, p. 10.

" emphasised by the individual vote of every lodge " connected
with the board, and was " regarded by " themselves " as a full
" confirmation of the justice of the sliding scale, and its permanent
" acceptance by the operatives as a written law to guide and
" regulate future wages."

The settlement of wages then by sliding scales has been
repeatedly abandoned in the manufactured iron trade of the north
of England. In the majority of cases this result has been produced because it has been contended by the one party or the other,
that other circumstances besides the mere selling prices should be
taken into consideration. Sometimes it is the relative position of
the ironworkers in other districts to which appeal is thus made;
sometimes it is the condition of the labour market; sometimes an
alteration in the cost of materials and the nature of the trade,
and sometimes the unfairness of the particular relation of wages to
selling prices on which the scale was originally based. The last of
these contentions will occupy our consideration in a little while.
At present we are concerned with the other three, and they may
be practically resolved into two, the one being the cost of materials,
and the other the state of the labour market.

(b). It is hardly necessary at this stage to argue that the
arrangement which is to form the basis of the scale must be in
accord with the traditions of the trade to which it is to apply, and
must rest on a common agreement. If then these elements have
been allowed to have weight in the past, they ought also to be
considered in the establishment of a sliding scale for the future.
From an economic point of view indeed there is considerable
reason for having regard to them, but it is the traditions of the
trade which are of the greatest importance. For the existence of
combinations on either side banishes, as we have noticed, to a very
great extent all economic considerations, so far at least as the
determination of the exact basis of the settlement is concerned.
The two parties do, it is true, stand towards one another in the
position of buyer and seller of a commodity, and that commodity is
labour. There is little, if any, trace of the old mediæval relation
between master and men—between the craftsman working at his
trade in his own house, and his journeymen and apprentices living
with him and eating at his table. It is of little use to sigh for the
revival of that relation, and it may even be questioned whether
" distance " has not lent " enchantment to the view " in this—as in
so many other cases—and whether that old relation did not possess
as full a share of disadvantages as that which is supposed to belong
to the " cash-nexus " of modern industry. But, though the two
parties have thus exchanged friendly, and in some respects even
paternal, relations for relations of strict business, yet the nego-

tiations into which they enter can hardly be reduced to a question
of pure economics, nor is there any economic touchstone which can
be brought into requisition to decide the matter.

In a certain sense, indeed, it may be said that the regulation of
wages by selling prices does rest upon an economic basis, however
the particular details of that basis may be arranged. It is in a
measure in accord with the theory of wages, which starts not from
a predetermined fund of capital accumulated in the past, and
fore-ordained to be employed in the remuneration of labour,
but—recognising the necessity of capital—from the price of the
product, or more strictly the total amount of wealth produced, as
the price of the product really means in the last analysis the
amount of wealth which can be obtained in exchange for it. But
it is to be noticed that the prices on which the wages are to be
based under a sliding scale are the realised prices of a previous
period, and not the prices "realisable" for the period during
which the wages are to be actually paid. The rates of wages then
may not be directly related to the price of the actual commodity
for the production of which they are paid. And the economic
theory of distribution, again, takes into consideration the question
of the supply of labour and the demand for its services as well
as the total amount of wealth produced; and this element is not
explicitly recognised in sliding scales. It may well be that circumstances may arise which "cause labour to be low" in price while
the "product" of labour is "relatively high," or which tend to
produce a contrary result;[302] and the economic theory of wages
takes account of this fact, while the sliding scale seems to ignore
it.[303] On the other hand there is considerable truth in the contention of the employers in the iron trade to which Sir Joseph Pease
alludes in one of his awards. "As[304] the article manufactured,"
they argued, "advanced in price by the action of the laws of
" supply and demand, so would the desire to create the profitable
" article occasion a greater demand for, and a consequent improved
" price for, the labour which produced it ; and " "thus the scale
" produced by its gradations the correct figure for the payment of
" the item of labour." Nor must we forget that the sliding scale
is to some extent originally fixed upon a competitive basis, and
that it is "historically" connected with competition so far as the
action of competition has not been affected by combination or
arbitration. It starts from a time when wages are to some extent
settled by competition, or at least, through the medium of combination, by the condition of the labour market. There may moreover
be—and as a matter of fact there have been—readjustments from

302 Cf. K, p. 36.   303 Cf. I. R. C. Report, p. 33.
304 Cf. IV, p. 23.

time to time of the regulations of the scales, if the circumstances of the trade or the labour market have conspicuously altered.[395] Thus a scale is not entirely divorced from competition, though it is certainly based upon traditions of trade rather than conclusions of economic science. In one colliery, indeed, Professor Munro states[396] that he has been told that " higher rates than those allowed by the " scale have been paid on account of the scarcity of miners."

With regard to the variation of other elements besides wages in the cost of production, there is comparatively little else to consider in the case of coal and iron mining save the selling price of the coal and iron. But in a manufacturing industry the cost of the raw material is also an appreciable element; and it is evident that a rise in prices by no means carries with it the ability to pay higher wages, if there is an equivalent—or more than equivalent— rise in the cost of the raw material. Here then there are elements in the cost of production, over and above wages, which can hardly be neglected with impunity; and the Derby sliding scale of 1874 in the manufactured iron trade of the north of England is said by the employers to have been arranged on a different basis from that of 1871, because of the increased cost of materials—of coal and of iron.[397] But there is no reason why this element should not be taken into consideration in framing the arrangements of a sliding scale, unless indeed it be an apprehension of complicating the scale by the introduction of too many variable elements. Such a difficulty as this, however—practically important as it undoubtedly is, and likely as it seems to delay the actual recognition of the point—is by no means insuperable; and it is surely because the principle of the sliding scale holds out such great promise of adaptation to these different contingencies, that Professor Munro has described[398] it as "the greatest discovery in the distribution of " wealth since Ricardo's enunciation of the law of rent." He strongly advocates its application to rent, and he notices the fact that the septennial average adopted in the payment of tithes is based upon a similar principle. A sliding scale, he urges,[399] may, and ought to, take into account those elements in the cost of production which are subject to considerable variations. It may

[395] Cf. I, p. 10. Since these lines were written the Northumberland coal owners have given the notice requisite for the determination of their scale, and demanded a reduction of 15 per cent. in wages (December, 1886).
[396] Cf. " Sliding Scales in the Coal Industry," p. 19.
[397] Cf. IV, p. 9.
[398] Cf. " Sliding Scales in the Iron Industry," p. 26. It has been applied in some cases to royalties. Cf. " Report of Royal Commission on Depression of " Trade." Q. 2313—4, 3570, 3609, 11823—6, 12178—9, 12353, 12408,— and to railway rates, Q. 2609.
[399] Cf. op. cit., p. 4.

allow from the first for those which can be reduced to an average, but the others should be introduced, if possible, into the scale itself as governing factors.

One other consideration, it may be noticed in conclusion, is met, and completely met, so far as seems practicable, by the sliding scale. For there can be little doubt that the appreciation of gold is at present a disturbing factor[400] of no small magnitude in industrial relations, and that in some instances workmen exhibit a somewhat pertinacious insistance upon nominal wages to the neglect of real wages—upon wages expressed in terms of money, to the neglect of wages expressed in terms of commodities. It is equally certain that an employer, who has bought his raw material and entered into his contract for wages or other matters when prices are high, and is then compelled to sell his manufactured goods when prices have become lower, is placed at a serious disadvantage. But the automatic adjustment of wages to prices effected by a sliding scale entirely avoids the difficulty occasioned by a *general*[401] appreciation of gold; and it would tell in a similar way in favour of the workmen's fair demands, if the monetary disturbance were caused by a *general* rise in prices and a depreciation in the metal adopted as the standard of value.

(c). But the difficulties of a sliding scale are not entirely over-come when the general character of the basis on which it is to rest has been settled. For, supposing that the relation between wages and selling prices is adopted as the basis, it then becomes necessary to agree upon a period when this relation is acknowledged to be in a normal condition. A time must be selected when, with the consent of both parties, wages bear a " fair " relation to prices ; and the prices realised at that time are regarded as the "standard" prices, and the wages then paid are the " standard " wages. With this as a starting point changes in wages are to follow fluctuations in prices,—whether upwards or downwards—whether in advances or reductions. But this agreement upon a fair and normal relation is by no means easy of attainment ; and the history of arbitration in the iron trade of the north abundantly illustrates this.[402] And, even when the two parties have arrived at an agreement, the same history proves that a change of considerable magnitude in the circumstances of the industry may necessitate the substitution of a new relation for that originally adopted.

---

[400] *Cf.* " Third Report of Royal Commission on the Depression of Trade," Appendix B ; and C.

[401] So far indeed as a fall or rise of prices can be said to be "general," in the sense of affecting with exact similarity the exchange of all commodities. *Cf. ibid.*, p. 423.

[402] *Cf. supra*, p. 69.

When this point has been satisfactorily settled, it becomes necessary to determine how often prices are to be ascertained, and wages revised; and this point may also give rise to dissension. A period must be taken which is not so brief as to imperil that stability of wages which is one of the chief benefits of a sliding scale, or, on the other hand, so protracted as to give to one side or the other, as the case may be from time to time, an excessive advantage, and thus to menace the other chief benefit of a scale—the stability of trade.[403] Another question has then to be settled. How great a variation in prices is to be held necessary to warrant a corresponding variation in wages? Here again an interval must be fixed which will fulfil the same two conditions as those just mentioned; and here the interval actually adopted varies in the coal mining industry from $1\frac{1}{2}d$. in Cumberland to $4\frac{1}{2}d$. under the Ocean scale, and in the Somerset scale every rise or fall in prices is to carry with it a rise or fall in wages.[404] Under the Cleveland scale[405] the interval is $0\cdot96d$. per ton for the ironstone miners, &c., and for the blast-furnace men it was 1s. In the manufactured iron trade of the north of England, and apparently also in that of Staffordshire, the interval was not less than 5s.[406]

Nor must it be forgotten that the amount of the corresponding variation in wages has also to be determined; and this may proceed according to an uniform succession—the same amount of variation taking place at each successive stage—or a principle of graduation may be introduced. Thus under the Durham scale of 1884 the usual variation is to be $1\frac{1}{4}$ and 1 per cent. in wages for every 2d. in prices, but for the interval of prices between 5s. 10d. and 6s. 2d. the variation in wage is to be twice the ordinary rate.[407] Somewhat similar are the provisions of the Northumberland scale of 1879, by which an extra rise of $2\frac{1}{2}$ and 2 per cent. of wages is contemplated for every advance of 1s. 4d. in prices, in addition to the ordinary variation of $2\frac{1}{2}$ and 2 per cent. of wages for every 4d. of prices; and the scale of 1883 allows this extra rise at certain prices specially named in the agreement.[408] In the iron industry the Cleveland scale adopts a similar course.[409] Under the Cumberland scale,[410] the

[403] The difficulty at present experienced with reference to the payment of tithe may be partly ascribed to the fact that the arrangements of the "sliding "scale" in this instance do not allow of a sufficiently *rapid* and *palpable* adjustment of tithe-payment to *existing* selling-prices.
[404] *Cf.* "Sliding Scales in the Coal Industry," p. 9.
[405] *Cf.* "Sliding Scales in the Iron Industry," p. 6.
[406] *Cf. op. cit.,* pp. 10 and 16; IX, p. 5.
[407] *Cf.* "Sliding Scales in the Coal Industry," p. 26.
[408] *Cf. op. cit.,* pp. 28 and 29.
[409] *Cf.* "Sliding Scales in the Iron Industry," p. 7.
[410] *Cf.* "Sliding Scales in the Coal Industry," pp. 33, 44, and 48.

Ocean scale, and partly also under the Ferndale scale, the contrary
principle is followed, and a lower percentage is recognised when
prices are high. But Professor Munro thinks[411] that this principle
is "unsound," and argues that if it be acknowledged that "wages
" are as much entitled as profits to share in the benefit" of
increased prices, the percentage ought to increase rather than
diminish. Such an arrangement, however, may be made, as in
the case of the Ferndale scale, in consideration of a change of the
basis of the scale in favour of the men.[412] But Professor Munro's
answer[413] to this plea is very cogent, when he urges that in such
instances the " scale has not been constructed on a sound economic
" basis." Or again, the concession may be made to counterbalance
the recognition of a minimum wage—a principle which is recognised in the Ocean scale.[414] This condition of a minimum wage
prevails also in the Bedworth scale, and, together with a maximum,
in the Somerset scale.[415] It was introduced into the first Durham
scale,[416] but there it seems to have occasioned no little dissatisfaction, and consequently to have been abandoned in succeeding
arrangements. In the manufactured iron trade the same principle
was inserted in 1881, in the Staffordshire scale of 1880, and retained
in the scale of 1883, which lasted for the brief period of six months.[417]
In the north of England difficulty seems to have arisen in the
course of the negotiations[418] conducted in 1885 upon the question
of the revival of the sliding scale, because the men insisted upon
a minimum wage ; and on other occasions they maintain that as
wages have not in the history of the trade followed prices up to
the highest level, so they ought not to follow them down to the
lowest point. If then this principle of a minimum be introduced—
and it is, we must remember, one of the cardinal points of a
trades unionist policy—it seems but a natural consequence that a
graduation in favour of the employers when prices are high should
also be introduced. On this point however we must not lose
sight of the consideration to which Professor Munro has drawn
attention. He shows that the migration of labour, so far as it is
operative, tends to establish an *economic* minimum ; for, if wages
fall below this, men will then migrate to other trades where the
rate of remuneration, allowing for advantages and disadvantages,
is higher than that which they are themselves receiving. And this
point is tacitly recognised[419] by the men in the iron trade in their
arguments before the arbitrator upon this very question of a
minimum wage.

[411] *Cf. op. cit.,* p. 10.
[412] *Cf. op. cit.,* p. 48.   [413] *Cf. op. cit.,* p. 10.   [414] *Cf. op. cit.,* p. 44.
[415] *Cf. op. cit.,* p. 50.   [416] *Cf. op. cit.,* p. 21.
[417] *Cf.* " Sliding Scales in the Iron Industry," pp. 16 and 17.
[418] *Cf.* VI, p. 17 ; IX, p. 4.   [419] *Cf.* I, p. 15 ; IX, p. 12.

CHAPTER V.

INDUSTRIAL CIRCUMSTANCES FAVOURING PEACE.

(A). The third and last difficulty attaching to sliding scales is that possibility of departure from the arrangement which menaces the success of all methods of conciliation and arbitration. The exact legal validity of the agreement on which a scale is based is a nice point in theory, and apparently has not as yet been defined in practice. The question resolves itself into a moral rather than a legal obligation, and the strength of that moral obligation depends upon the representative character of the negotiating parties. The same difficulty exists, as we have seen,[420] in all cases of conciliation and arbitration, and it seems to be most satisfactorily met by the organisation of trades unions. Hence it is a question of no little interest to ascertain the number of trades unionists, and the proportion which they bear in each instance to the total number of workmen engaged in any particular industry. But upon this point it is hardly possible to arrive at any but the most general conclusions, whether we start from the one side or from the other. For, on the one hand, that portion of the Census which relates to the Occupations of the people is confessedly very inaccurate;[421] and the returns must be accepted with the greatest caution. If, on the other hand, we commence our inquiry with the number of trades unionists, we have only imperfect, and in some instances approximate, figures on which to rely. If we take the returns of the Registrar, we have to recollect that registration is voluntary, and that there may be societies which are not willing to conform with the registration regulations. Mr. George Howell, who is probably more intimately acquainted with the inner working of trades unions than any other writer upon the subject, stated,[422] in October, 1882, that there were some 177 societies included in the Chief Registrar's returns, but that it was likely that there were not less than 600 " independent societies " in Great Britain. If again

---

[420] *Cf. supra*, pp. 14 and 82.
[421] *Cf.* Census returns, vol. iv; general report, sec. vi.
[422] *Cf.* " Nineteenth Century," October, 1882, " The Financial Condition of " Trades Unions."

we were to endeavour to gather information by the toilsome method of collecting together trades union reports, we should at once be arrested by the insuperable obstacle that some societies do not issue reports, and that in many cases the reports are merely published for internal circulation.

The best information to be procured upon the point seems to be that contained in the reports of the annual trades union congresses,[423] to which are prefixed the names and addresses of the delegates attending the congress from the various societies, together with the number of the members which they represent. But even here we must not forget that some societies do not send delegates, and that the numbers seem to be only approximate.[424] Nor are our difficulties at an end when we have reached this point. For suppose that we take for example the Boiler-makers and Iron Shipbuilders' Union, with a membership of 28,500, according to the congress report for 1885, and of 28,212, or 27,695, according to the annual report of the society itself. If we then turn to the census returns for England and Wales for 1881, and endeavour to find out the total number of workmen engaged in these occupations, we can indeed ascertain the number of so-called "boilermakers" (26,170), but when we look at the heading of "shipbuilders" (21,741), we are told that it includes the builders of boats and barges as well as of ships. Or, to take another illustration, according to the congress report, the Amalgamated Association of Operative Cotton Spinners includes 16,115 members; but the census returns add together into one sum all the workers engaged in some of the chief branches of the cotton industry, and at any rate do not distinguish between spinners and weavers. In the iron industry, once more, the Ironfounders' Friendly Society of England, Ireland, and Wales has a membership of 12,410, the Associated Iron Moulders of Scotland number 5,500, and the National Amalgamated Association of Iron and Steel Workers records a muster-roll of 2,000 members. But here the census returns for England and Wales are very vague, and merely enumerate "iron and steel workers;" and apparently it is only "nail makers" and "chain

---

[423] *Cf.* "Trades Union Congress Report," 1885, pp. 1—6.

[424] According to the "Trades Union Congress Report" for 1885, the number of the Boilermakers and Iron shipbuilders is 28,500; but according to the annual report of the society itself for 1885 it is in the summary table 28,212; and in the secretary's report dated 17th March, 1886, in which a decrease of 1,200 during the year is noticed, it is 27,695.
Cf. "Trades Union Congress Report for 1885," p. 1; "Report of the Boiler-makers' Society," pp. xi and xii. Similarly the Amalgamated Engineers are put down in the Congress Report as 51,000, and in their own annual report, issued in May, 1886, as 51,689, and as 50,681 at the close of 1884.
Cf. "Trades Union Congress Report," p. 2; "Newcastle Daily Leader," 7th May, 1886.

ITS ADVANTAGES, METHODS, AND DIFFICULTIES.   101

" and anchor makers " who are specially distinguished. Or again,
take the case of plumbers and tailors. The census returns may
include master-plumbers and master-tailors, and enumerate in the
one case 37,400, in the other 160,648. But the United Operative
Society of Plumbers of Great Britain and Ireland numbers 2,645,
and the Amalgamated Society of Tailors 15,378.

Thus we can at the best arrive at merely general results.
Mr. George Howell, for example, states[125] that in "a few instances"
the proportion of society to non-society men amounts to two-thirds,
or even three-fourths, of the workmen in a trade; that the general
ratio is one-third society men to two-thirds non-society men; and
that, even to command one-third of the workmen in a trade
throughout the length and breadth of the country, the trade must
be "exceedingly well organised."

There seems moreover to be a capriciousness about the growth
of trades unionism not unlike that which characterises co-operation;
and it may be noticed in passing that the two movements may
almost be said to be coincident in the general mass of their leaders
and adherents. An official of one of the trades councils in the
north of England informed me that the principles of unionism were
strong in Lancashire, weak in the Midlands, and fairly vigorous in
the North.[126] A similar fluctuation of strength is apparent between
trade and trade; although in this case also, for the reasons we have
previously mentioned, our conclusions must be of a general
character. The miners appear on the whole to be well organised,
and the successful establishment of sliding scales is no small
evidence of this. In Northumberland and Durham not only do the
Miners' Associations number respectively 12,500 and 20,000, but
in the former county there is also a Mutual Aid Association formed
by the Deputies, and numbering 475, and a Colliery Enginemen
and Firemen's Mutual Protection Association, with a total membership of 406 ;[127] and in the latter[128] the Durham Enginemen's Association, numbering 1,258, the Durham Colliery Mechanics' Association,
numbering 2,000, and the Durham Cokemen's Association, numbering 1,500, are expressly named as parties to the agreements for the
scales of 1879, 1882, and 1884, in addition to the Coal Owners'
Association and the Miners' Association. The Amalgamated Association of Operative Cotton Spinners has a membership of 16,115
or 16.500, and is stated[129] by the secretary in his evidence before
the Royal Commission on the Depression of Trade, to include
" nearly the whole of the grown up men " that are in the trade—

[125] Cf. "Nineteenth Century," October, 1882.
[126] Cf. I, p. 14.
[127] Cf. "Newcastle Daily Leader," 1st February, 1886.
[128] Cf. "Sliding Scales in the Coal Industry," pp. 22, 24, and 26.
[129] Cf. Second Report, Q. 5038, 5059; part ii, Appendix D, p. 72, ans. 3.

the balance of the 54,000 operatives or so engaged in the cotton
spinning industry consisting of "young persons" and "children."
The Northern Counties Amalgamated Association of Weavers
numbers 40,000, the Amalgamated Society of Carpenters and
Joiners 25,750, the Operative Masons' Society 12,000, and the
National Union of Boot and Shoe Riveters and Finishers 10,317,
according to the congress report. But according to the same
report the Operative Bricklayers' Society only reaches the figure
of 6,069 members, and the United Operative Plumbers' Association
that of 2,645 members. The evidence furnished by the membership of the different trades councils exhibits a similar fluctuation,
although we must remember in this case that the councils are voluntary organisations—as indeed the unions themselves theoretically
are—and that therefore they must be regarded as indications of the
vigour of unionist principles rather than of the actual number of
unionists. In Oldham the council represents 10,000, in Manchester
7,000, but in Leicester only 1,950, and in Newcastle 2,000. In the
last place indeed it is a curious fact that, according to a statement[130] made by Mr. Laird, the president of the Newcastle Trades'
Council, at the congress of 1885, "about two-thirds" of the men
employed at the well known ordnance and engine works of Sir
William G. Armstrong, Mitchell, and Co., who came out of work
in consequence of a strike in the autumn of that year, "belonged to
" no association at all."

A casual glance at the answers furnished by the officials of
different trade societies to certain questions addressed to them by
the Royal Commission on the Depression of Trade,[131] will supply
confirmatory evidence of the varying strength of trades unions.

The Secretary of the local branch of the Amalgamated
Engineers at Belfast writes,[132] "we could form no idea of the
" number of non-society men employed;" and the local secretary
of the same society at Neath says,[133] "our own members number
" about 32, but I should think there must be at least four or five
" times the number non-society men, but this is a guess only, and
" not to be relied on." The Hartlepool secretary of the Boilermakers and Iron Shipbuilders reports[134] that there would be
" about as many more" men as he has mentioned "connected with
" the trade, but unconnected with his society;" while in the Tees
district it appears from the answers[135] of the Stockton secretary
that there are no "non-members." The secretary of the Iron-

[130] Cf. Report, p. 43.
[131] Cf. Second Report, part ii, Appendix D.
[132] Cf. Report, part ii, Appendix D, p. 7.
[133] Cf. op. cit., p. 11.   [134] Cf. op. cit., p. 18.
[135] Cf. op. cit., p. 19.

founders at Derby states[436] that there are "212 society men
"engaged in his trade in his district, and about the same number
"of non-society men." The Leeds secretary of the Loyal Free
Industrious Society of Wheelwrights and Blacksmiths says,[437] that
"about eight to one" do "not belong to our society." The general
secretary of the United Pattern-Makers' Association supplies[438]
some figures relating to the Glasgow district, which show
250 pattern-makers belonging to his society, 150 to "other
"societies," and 400 to "no society at all." The Wolverhampton
secretary of the Tin Plate Workers reports[439] that 340 men belong
to his society, and that about 100 do not. In the case of the
Operative Bricklayers' Society, the secretary for Ironbridge says[440]
that it is "impossible to ascertain the exact number" of workmen
in his trade in his district, "as there are a very large number
"unconnected with the society;" and in the case of the Operative
Stonemasons' Friendly Society the Doncaster secretary refers[441] to
a "few non-society men," the Newcastle-upon-Tyne secretary[442]
gives a proportion of "400 society-masons to about 100 non-
"society men," and the Nottingham secretary[443] of 150 masons in
"the society" to "about 50 not in" the society. In the case of
the Amalgamated Society of Carpenters and Joiners, the Cardiff
secretary reports[444] "100 (or 120?) non-society men," to 120
"society men;" and the Hammersmith secretary writes[445] that the
members of his society are "unfortunately" "in the minority" in
London. The Manchester secretary of the General Union of
Operative Carpenters and Joiners notices[446] a defection from their
own ranks to those of the Amalgamated Society, and adds that
"a great many are out of society altogether." The Liverpool secretary of the United Operative Plumbers' Association reports[447]
"about 300 non-union men" to "240 union men;" and the
London secretary of the Amalgamated Society of Gilders states[448]
that there are 150 men "in the society," "about double that
"number" outside the society in the West End, and "about
"double the combined number of society and non-society men
"in the East End." In the case of the Typographical Association, in the last place, we find the Halifax secretary referring[449]
to "36 members," and "probably about a similar number" "who
"are not members;" and the Huddersfield secretary states[450] that

[436] Cf. op. cit., p. 22.
[437] Cf. op. cit., p. 33.
[439] Cf. op. cit., p. 41.
[441] Cf. op. cit., p. 48.
[443] Cf. op. cit., p. 50.
[445] Cf. op. cit., p. 57.
[447] Cf. op. cit., p. 66.
[449] Cf. op. cit., p. 82.
[438] Cf. op. cit., p. 40.
[440] Cf. op. cit., p. 43.
[442] Cf. op. cit., p. 50.
[444] Cf. op. cit., p. 54.
[446] Cf. op. cit., p. 64.
[448] Cf. op. cit., p. 69.
[450] Cf. op. cit., p. 83.

" Trades Unionists' principles are very weak in this district in
" our trade."

A few isolated indications may also be gathered from the
evidence actually given before the commissioners. Thus it appears
that, "with few exceptions," trades unions are "not at all in
" a flourishing condition in Sheffield at the present time.[451] At
Leeds "there are some associations controlling the action of the
" weavers," but the woollen industry is "perhaps freer than most
" from associations of that kind, owing to the variety of work
" which is involved in the woollen manufacture."[452] At Bradford, where the work is also diversified, it seems that "there is
" no trade union connected with the staple industries of the
town,"[453] and at Macclesfield[454] the silk manufacturers express
their satisfaction at the practical disappearance of trades unions
from their town and industry. On the Clyde again a "considerable
" number of engineers" and a certain amount of the iron ship-
" building class, do not" belong to the unions.[455]

(B). The variety of detail in the trade, to which the manufacturers of Leeds and of Bradford refer in their evidence before the
commission, may present hindrances to the organisation of trades
unions. But it has not by any means proved fatal to conciliation;
for the success of the principle in the hosiery trades of the
Midlands has been conspicuous. And yet here—as has been
shown in a paper read before the British Association at Dundee
in 1867—[456] there was as much diversity of minute detail as
could well be conceived. There was variety of goods, variety of
prices, and variety of workers. This diversity of detail is quite
consistent also with the institution and the successful working
of a sliding scale; and as a matter of actual fact local variations
in wages are recognised in the coal and iron industries to
which the principle has been so successfully applied. Jevons
indeed ,goes so far as to maintain[457] that conciliation is likely
to be more successful where the multiplicity of detail is greater;
for in these cases the necessity of some arrangement—some
schedule of prices—must be obvious to the dullest observer.
Nor is the absence of trades unions so valid an objection to a
system of conciliation as to present insuperable obstacles to its
success. For a rudimentary form of organised representation may

[451] Cf. Second Report, Q. 2914 and 2725.
[452] Cf. op. cit., Q. 6317.   [453] Cf. op. cit., Q. 3976—7.
[454] Cf. op. cit., Q. 7239—12, 7394, and 7493.
[455] Q. 12020. Cf. also Q. 12105.
[456] Cf. Statistical Society's Journal, vol. xxx, December, 1867, pp. 518—56,
Arbitration in the Hosiery Trades of the Midland Counties, by E. Renals. Cf.
also Report by J. D. Weeks, sec. iii, p. 5, &c.
[457] Cf. "State in Relation to Labour," p. 156.

conceivably prove to be an efficient substitute for an union, so far as the regulation of wages is concerned.

And, on the other hand, the presence of an union is not an absolutely sure guarantee for the success of principles of conciliation. For, in the first place, there is a difference in industries. Some, like the cotton and woollen trades, are localised in a high degree; some again are settled in different centres, such as the engineering, the shipbuilding, and the mining industries; some may be found in every town, and in this class we may place the building, the printing, and the domestic trades. If then there is only a comparatively small number of men located in a particular district, the trades union organisation does not seem to secure the undoubted advantage of effecting negotiations on behalf of a large body through the medium of a few representatives. It would rather be necessary, it appears, to create a number of little boards of conciliation, and to institute a number of minute sliding scales in each district; and this might entail considerable expense. But, on the other hand, it is conceivable that the representative system might effect a solution of this difficulty; and the general arrangements of a sliding scale may, as we have seen, admit of almost innumerable local diversities and sectional adaptations. And so the advantage of the official experience and influence of the central executive may perhaps on a representative basis be satisfactorily combined with local variety of detail. The difficulty then of instituting a system of conciliation is certainly increased by these circumstances, but it is not rendered insuperable. Where indeed the industry, though diffused in different centres, is yet concentrated in considerable strength in particular localities—like the manufactured iron trade, and the shipbuilding trade, and to some extent also the engineering trade— this difficulty is reduced to a minimum. For the case is assimilated for all practical purposes to that of industries which are highly localised; and as a matter of actual fact boards of conciliation have been formed in the iron trades of the north of England and of Staffordshire, and even in the building trades at Wolverhampton and Birmingham.

In the second place, it may be stated as a general truth that the success of the conciliatory system is most likely to be secured where there is at the very beginning a kindly feeling between masters and men, and that it is more probable that those feelings will be engendered where the same men come into contact with the same masters, and the general body of men and masters is not always changing in its component parts. It must not however be forgotten that the relations of masters and men in the manufactured iron trade of the north of England seem to have

been of the most unfriendly description before the institution of
the board of conciliation, and yet the board has undoubtedly been
a conspicuous success. In the Northumberland coal trade also,
despite of the friendliness existing between masters and men for
several years—a friendliness to which frequent reference had been
made before arbitrators, and a friendliness which had for long
secured the peaceful settlement of industrial relations by amicable
negotiation—that friendliness was strained to the utmost immediately before the introduction of the sliding scale. These facts
are sufficient to warn us against a despondent and hopeless
inactivity, although they do not seem to affect the general correct-
ness of the statement we have advanced.

(c). i. An industry in which there is considerable migration—
both into and out of its ranks—or one within the ranks of which
there is frequent migration from place to place—whether it be
from district to district, or from shop to shop—is not an industry
in which permanent relations are likely to be established between
masters and men. Hence it becomes a matter of no small interest
to ascertain the leading characteristics of the industrial society of
modern England in this respect. But the difficulty of the inquiry
is as unmistakable as is its interesting nature. We can only hope
to arrive at the most general conclusions.

Examination of industrial society has shown that there are considerable hindrances to the "mobility of labour" from place to
place, and from occupation to occupation, if we interpret the phrase
in the extravagant sense sometimes given to it by unfair opponents
of the "orthodox" school. Cairnes has, however, finally shown[454]
that, to establish the validity of the "orthodox" theory, it is not
necessary to prove that every particular fraction of capital, and
every individual labourer, should possess the ability and the wish
to migrate to any place or any industry where economic advantage
would lead. But it is only requisite that a certain amount of
capital, and a certain amount of labour—enough to establish the
correspondence of abstinence and labour to their remuneration—
should possess this characteristic. Capital, he maintains, does
exhibit the requisite amount of mobility from occupation to
occupation, but labour does not. Following, with apparent
unconsciousness, in the lines laid down by Mill,[459] he divides
economic society into four rough classes, which may be briefly

[454] *Cf.* "Some Leading Principles of Political Economy," by J. E. Cairnes.
I, iii, 5. *Cf.* also, so far as capital is concerned, Ricardo's "Principles of
Political Economy and Taxation," ch. iv; J. S. Mill's "Principles of Political
Economy," II, xv, 4.
[459] *Cf.* "Principles of Political Economy," by J. S. Mill. II, xiv, 2;
III, iv, 3. *Cf.*, however, "Some Leading Principles," I, iii, 3; edition 1885,
p. 53.

described as unskilled labour, the lower ranks and the higher ranks of skilled labour,—including in the former class small, and in the latter superior, retail traders,—and the professional and higher mercantile classes. He holds that there is sufficient mobility of labour within each group—not indeed of men actually engaged in any industry, but of youthful labour constantly growing up and seeking the most remunerative employment—to establish the truth of the orthodox theory of value as applied to the mutual exchange of the products of its labour alone; but that these groups themselves are "non-competing" in the sense that competition, active within the limits of any one of them, is not able to exercise its equalising effects to any practical extent beyond these limits.

Professor Walker[460] has adopted the same general position, but he has modified it in such a manner that his attitude seems to be really more akin to that of Mill. On the one hand he does not allow that competition and mobility cease for all "practical" purposes, when they reach the limits of these "non-competing" groups; nor on the other hand does he recognise the existence of "perfect" mobility within these boundaries. And this seems to be the most tenable position. It would be rash to contend that there is "perfect" mobility of labour, or indeed, for that matter, of capital, in modern society; but it does not for that reason appear to be true, as Professor Ingram[461] seems to agree with Cliffe-Leslie in maintaining, that the economic theory of value must be constructed on an entirely fresh basis, by the aid of careful and wide induction, and the most intimate connection with a science of sociology which has indeed still to be created. We must have a hypothesis from which to start—and to this Professor Ingram would himself assent—and the hypothesis of pure competition is the most convenient, and, indeed, may be said with some reason to be also the most secure.

But its hypothetical character must always be borne in mind, and its very security lies in the fact that it seems to be more difficult to forget this hypothetical character in its case, than it would·be if Cairnes' modification were generally adopted as a starting-point. Even in the economic world of "business men," even in the "great commerce" " as it is known in England," there are obstacles to the mobility of labour—whether it be the labour of employers or employed. But society does not on that

---

[460] Cf. "Wages Question," ch. XI. It is to be noticed that Cairnes disclaims for himself any intention to suppose that there is *rigidity* in the lines separating his non-competing groups; but his argument in some places might tend to create this impression.

[461] Cf. "Encyclopædia Britannica," 9th edit. Article on "Political Economy," by J. K. Ingram.

account seem to be divided into four groups—roughly defined as those groups may be—but rather into innumerable groups within groups. There does indeed appear to be one line of demarcation establishing itself, but that line does not seem to lie—as platform rhetoric is so fond of placing it—between the "working-classes" so called and the rest of society, so much as it does between skilled and unskilled labour. There does not appear to be any broad "economic gulf" yawning between the "rich" and the "poor;" but on the contrary—with the exception of this division between skilled and unskilled labour—class seems to run into class with almost indistinguishable lines. The working-classes, in all likelihood, contain as many classes within classes as do the professional and trading classes, and the "aristocracy" so called; and indeed a theory of non-competing groups—if we attempt to draw anything approaching to a hard and fast line at any particular point—really seems to be almost, if not quite, as much in conflict with actual fact as a theory of pure competition. The latter theory, indeed, as we said before, appears to be almost a safer guide, for it is difficult to be blind to its hypothetical character; but the former theory may not impossibly mislead by an appearance of conformity to actual fact. Economic motives and influences then seem to be present in most cases, although they can only be detected in their broad tendencies, and although now, as in the past, they meet with many obstacles, arising in some cases from ignorance, in some from poverty, and in some from the *vis inertiæ* of custom and habit.

ii. (*a*). Let us take first the question of migration from place to place. There is a quotation upon this point which has become almost proverbial. "A man is of all sorts of luggage the most difficult to be transported," wrote[162] Adam Smith more than a hundred years ago; and even in these days of cheapened travelling the words contain a world of truth. The only addition which at first sight it appears ought to be made, is that a woman is yet more difficult than a man. For there are fewer occupations open to her, and her sex is, in the nature of things, more likely to be fettered in its movements. But—surprising as it may seem—the census returns actually show that "woman is a greater migrant "than man."[163]

This result, however, it would seem, must be attributed in the main to the movements, not of married but of unmarried women

---

[162] *Cf.* "Wealth of Nations," by Adam Smith, book I, ch. viii, p. 34. McCulloch's edition, 1863.
[163] *I.e.*, within the limits of the *kingdom* of her birth. *Cf.* Statistical Society's *Journal*, vol. xlviii, part ii, June, 1885. "The Laws of Migration," by E. G. Ravenstein, p. 196.

and widows, and to the large numbers of women who are engaged as domestic servants.[464] For a married woman is naturally tied to her husband and her family; and this is a fact which is sometimes forgotten in considering the economic theory of the mobility of labour. That theory only assumes that labour will move when it secures a distinct economic advantage by so doing. But in estimating relative advantages we must remember that the family must be taken as the true unit of working-power, and the family income as the unit of wages; and that it may happen, for instance, that a man may secure higher earnings for himself by moving from Leeds to Newcastle, and yet it may not be for his "economic" advantage to do this, because in Leeds his wife and daughters could earn money as machinists as well as himself, and in Newcastle there would be comparatively very little opening for female labour.

Nor, again, in the case of an individual man, is it easy to estimate exactly the comparative advantages and disadvantages of different places, or, indeed, of different occupations. It is difficult to reduce "money wages" to their exact equivalent in "real "wages." An agricultural labourer[465] may move from Roxburghshire to Newcastle, and think that he will secure higher remuneration. But when he arrives he may find that he is really in a worse position, and may return to his former home, where he earns in actual cash, it is true, perhaps not more than 12s. or 14s. a week, but receives in addition in all probability a free cottage, coals, the use of a cow, the keep of a pig, some yards of potatoes, and a month's provisions at harvest. It would be easy to multiply instances of this nature; but it seems clear, without any further proof, that unless the economic advantage to be secured by a move is very distinct—and this was clearly pointed out by Adam Smith in the case of movement from occupation to occupation—the move is not, as a general rule, likely to be made, although in this, as in other cases, imagination may exaggerate, and fancy delude.

And even in the presence of this distinct advantage there may be feelings of such a character that they cannot be easily reduced to an economic standard, which hinder—and naturally hinder— the mobility of labour. The love of home—as expressed by the people who think "there's nee place like Walker,"[466] and attachment to friends, present obstacles which few could wish removed. Mr. Ravenstein, relying upon the census returns of 1881, has

<hr/>

[464] Mr. Ravenstein states, however, that the "workshop is a formidable rival "of the kitchen and scullery." P. 196.

[465] Cf. "Wages Question," ch. II, p. 22. There seems to be a tendency to substitute money wages for these allowances in Northumberland at any rate. Cf. Report of the Royal Commission on the Depression of Trade. Q. 8688.

[466] Walker is one of the villages on Tyneside.

attempted[467] to arrive at general "laws of migration"—as he calls
them—and his conclusions confirm the power of this love of home.
He made a similar examination[468] of the returns of 1871, but in
both cases the results present the same general characteristics.
Migration is by no means inconsiderable, and seems indeed to be
more extensive than might have been imagined; but in the cases
where it can be traced it is apparently to no great distance that the
migrants remove.   In 1881, out of 34,534,048 persons enumerated
as natives of the United Kingdom, no less than 25,762,415 were
living in the county of their birth, 4,049,918 in border-counties,
and 33,315,868 resided in the kingdom where they were born.
The manufacturing counties in England and Scotland, as might be
expected, attract the population from the agricultural counties;
and it is probably because Ireland is so largely agricultural that
migration within its borders is, in comparison with that in England
and Scotland, much more limited in extent.

But there is evidence that these migrants do not for the most
part continue their travels to any great distance.   The Irish, who
come in the largest numbers, not from the West, but apparently
from Ulster, Dublin, Wexford, and Cork (together with Kerry and
Limerick), seem to linger in the ports at which they have dis-
embarked.   These are of course in the main upon the West Coast
of England and Scotland; and it is apparently only by comparatively gradual degrees, and in small detachments, that they make
their way into the rest of the country, although there is not a
single county in Great Britain in which they are not found.   The
Scotch, again, are discovered in large numbers in the North of
England, and amount to as much as 5 per cent. in Northumberland,
and 4 per cent. in Cumberland, of the total population of those counties.   But, as we go southwards, the proportion diminishes to 2·85 per
cent. in Durham, 1·63 per cent. in Westmoreland, 1·62 per cent. in
Lancashire, 1·22 per cent. in Cheshire, and to 0·67 per cent. in
Yorkshire; and the case is similar with the English immigrants
into Scotland.   An examination, too, of particular districts exhibits
analogous features with regard to migration from county to
county and town to town.   The inhabitants of the country in the
immediate neighbourhood of a large town appear to migrate into
the town; their places seem to be taken by immigrants from
border districts and counties; their place again by immigrants who
have come from a greater distance; and in this manner, and

    [467] Cf. Statistical Society's *Journal*, vol. xlviii, part ii. "The Laws of
" Migration," by E. G. Ravenstein, pp. 168—227.
    [468] Cf. "The Birth-places of the People and the Laws of Migration."
Reprinted from the " Geographical Magazine, 1870."

according to laws which exhibit these general features, the tide of migration seems to ebb and flow.

It is interesting to find that Mr. Ravenstein selects the town of Middlesbrough as an illustration[469] of one of his points; and the instance is peculiarly instructive for our purpose, as it is connected with the rapid development of the Cleveland iron district. He shows how the population of Middlesbrough increased 108 per cent. between 1861 and 1871, and 40 per cent. between 1871 and 1881. In 1861 the proportion of the population of the city who were natives of the county of Yorkshire was 73·2 per cent.;[470] in 1871, owing to the immigration of iron-workers and miners from Durham, South Wales, Staffordshire, and Scotland, together with an influx of Irish labourers, it had sunk to 50·1 per cent.; and in 1881 it had risen to 55 in consequence of the diminution in the tide of immigrants and of the birth of children. But even in this case the chief volume of the tide when it was at its height came, apparently, from Yorkshire itself and the border-counties, although the population of Middlesbrough includes contingents from all the counties of England and Wales. Thus the population of the town amounted to 39,563 in 1871, and 55,934 in 1881; and of these in 1871, 50·1 per cent., and in 1881, 54·8 per cent. were, as we have seen, natives of Yorkshire; 13·3 per cent. in 1871, and 13·5 per cent. in 1881 came from the neighbouring county of Durham, and 2·4 in 1871 and 2·3 in 1881 from the more distant county of Northumberland. Ireland contributed a contingent of considerable magnitude: 9·1 in 1871 (although the proportion in 1861 had only been 2·0), and in 1881, 6·6. From the mining and ironworking districts of Staffordshire and Wales (together with Monmouthshire) came a proportion of 3·9 in 1871, and 3·0 in 1881 from the latter, and from the former 2·6 in 1871, and 2·1 in 1881. From Scotland, in the last place, 2·9 came in 1871, and 2·8 in 1881.

Hence there does not appear to be, comparatively speaking, a large amount of migration from *distant* place to *distant* place,— though there may indeed be more than sufficient even here to meet the conditions of the theory of value—save in those exceptional cases where a fresh industry starts into life in a district, or moves from an old to a new and more advantageous locality; and even in these cases the tide of immigration seems to flow in greatest volume from the neighbouring districts. But we must not forget

[469] Mr. Ravenstein points out that the " rapid growth," the " heterogeneous " composition of the population," and the " preponderance of the male sex " in the town, exhibit similar features to those commonly " credited only to the towns " of the American west."

[470] The registrar's " district of Guisborough " (22,128 inhabitants) is taken as representing the Middlesbrough (18,992 inhabitants) of 1861, as no other details of the birth-places for that year are " available."

the fact which is not indeed irreconcilable with this, and has been
brought into frequent prominence by the complaints of canvassers
in Parliamentary and municipal elections—when they urge that
their difficulties are increased by the extensive removal of voters
who were resident in the district a little while before, and have
left with their names still upon the registers.

(b) (1). Some industries, again, are naturally of a more migratory
character than others. For some industries are, as we saw before,
localised—either wholly or in part—in particular districts, and others
are scattered throughout the length and breadth of the country.

Thus—to take an instance of the first class—the cotton-spinning
industry is settled in Lancashire and the neighbouring counties of
Yorkshire, Cheshire, and Derbyshire; and consequently migration
outside the limits of this district would be an anomaly.   But
within its limits there seems to be considerable migration; for the
general secretary of the Amalgamated Association of Operative
Cotton Spinners writes[471] that the members of his society are

[471] Upon this and some other kindred points I addressed some inquiries to the
secretaries of different important trades unions; and the following is a list of
those from whom I have received answers. In the courteous letters which they
kindly sent to me in answer to my questions, they state in most instances that
they can only give me information of a "general character," based upon their
"experience" and "impressions":—

Number of Members Represented, according
   to Trades Union Congress Report, 1885.

25,750	Mr. J. S. Murchie	Secretary of the Amalgamated Society of Carpenters and Joiners.
16,115	Mr. J. Mawdsley	Secretary of the Amalgamated Society of Operative Cotton Spinners.
51,000	Mr. J. Burnett	late Secretary of the Amalgamated Society of Engineers.
28,500	Mr. R. Knight	Secretary of the United Society of Boiler-makers and Iron Shipbuilders.
10,317	Mr. G. Sedgwick	Secretary of the National Union of Boot and Shoe Riveters and Finishers.
1,500	Mr. T. Hart	Secretary of the Durham Cokemen's Association.
6,350	Mr. C. J. Drummond....	Secretary of the London Society of Compositors.
12,500	Mr. R. Young...............	Secretary of the Northumberland Miners' Mutual Confident Association.
6,388	Mr. H. Slatter	Secretary of the Typographical Association.
14,000	Mr. G. Mackay	Of the Trades Council, Edinburgh.
5,000	Mr. W. J. Strachan	„ Hull.
24,523	Mr. G. Shipton	„ London.
12,000	Mr. A. J. Hunter	„ Glasgow.

Besides these letters I have also had the advantage of personal interviews with
Mr. Edward Trow, Secretary of the National Amalgamated Association of Iron
and Steel Workers (2,000 members), and Mr. J. C. Laird, President of the Trades
Council, Newcastle-upon-Tyne (2,000 members), upon the subjects discussed in
this portion of the report.

" constantly moving about," and that he " should say that probably
" not one half lived in the same town all their lives," and in
" small towns and villages " this proportion would fall below " one
" fourth."

With regard to the second class of trades—those which are
localised indeed, but are settled in more than one district—there is
a general impression in the north of England—and the impression
seems to be substantiated by facts—about the miners, who form
the most numerous industry of this class, that the Northumbrian
miner is of a type quite distinct from that of the Durham miner,
although the river Tyne alone forms the chief boundary between
the two counties. The Northumbrian miner has been described[172]
by the owners themselves before parliamentary committees and
arbitrators as belonging to a " most advanced type of mankind,"
and to a body of men who are " very steady " and " do not move
" about." But in Durham there appears to be more of a foreign and
migratory element; and this difference, it is to be noticed, seems
to be partly due to the fact that the steam coal, which forms the
staple coal of the Northumbrian district, requires a higher amount
of skill than that needed in the case of other coal before it can be
properly worked. If, indeed, there be migration from the Northumbrian district, it appears to take the form of emigration to America
rather than that of migration to the other mining districts of
Great Britain. Within the district itself there seems to be some
movement, though not to any considerable extent. The secretary
of the Miners' Union writes that " from 5 to 7½ per cent. do not
" stay more than twelve months at a place, and 15 or 20 per cent.
" stay from fifteen to twenty years. The average residence at a
" place will be from seven to eight years."

He also alludes to a special cause in connection with the mining
industries of Northumberland and Durham which seems to affect
this percentage of migration; for in these two counties the miners
have an allowance in addition to wages in the shape of a house and
a certain amount of coals. But this house-accommodation is not
always sufficient to meet the requirements of all the colliers at a
particular pit; and in lieu of this the owners in some cases make
a money-grant, varying from 1s. to 2s. a week, and then the men
have to seek for a house where they can. But, as this allowance is
" usually " not more than " half the rent " that has to be paid,
these men are placed at a disadvantage in comparison with those
who enjoy the possession of free houses. They are consequently
eager—and Mr. Young says that there is a " considerable per-
" centage " of men in this situation at " nearly every colliery " in

172 *Cf.* K, pp. 2, 23, and 83.

I

Northumberland—to move to any colliery where they can obtain a
free house. And so, when a new colliery is opened or new houses
are built, there is certain to be an influx of labour to the place.
This point is worth noticing on more than one ground. For
here we have a distinct case of movement in search of economic
advantage, and yet that advantage would not be detected by any
external examination of the comparative rates of wages. And, in
the second place, the matter is intimately connected with a very
interesting and important question, which was raised by the late
Bishop of Manchester in a sermon preached before the Co-operative
Congress at Oldham in 1885. In that sermon Dr. Fraser suggested[473]
the doubt whether it was "always an advantage" for a working-
man to live in a house of his own; for in that case, should a sudden
change in the circumstances of industry compel him to seek
employment elsewhere, he might have to sell his house—perhaps at
a loss—or travel a long distance to and from his work. The
secretary, however, of one of the largest building societies[474] in
Newcastle—and in the local newspapers of that town may sometimes be seen the successive advertisements of seven or eight
building[475] societies appearing below one another in a single
column—writes that in his society, in which the range of monetary
advances extends "from London in the south to Cumberland in
" the west and North Northumberland " in the north, but "never
" crosses the border" into Scotland,[476] the "rank and file of build-
" ing society members in Newcastle consist chiefly of the business
" or middle class and the lower strata of tradesmen." "Very few
" of the working classes in proportion," he adds, "purchase their
" houses." "As a rule the working classes do not go in for
" purchasing or owning the houses they occupy. My experience
" is that they are more disposed to invest any moneys they can
" accumulate in Preference shares or Depository shares. In my
" society we have a considerable number investing with us in
" these two ways. They prefer investing their moneys at interest
" rather than in bricks and mortar, so that they can draw upon
" their reserve at any time without inconvenience or loss. In this

---

    [473] Cf. Co-operative Congress Report, p. 66.
    [474] I.e., the Grainger Permanent Building Society.
    [475] I.e., (1). The Tyne Commercial Permanent Building Society.
        (2). Monarch Building Society.
        (3). The Newcastle-upon-Tyne Permanent Building Society.
        (4) (?) The Old Established Building Societies Offices (sic).
        (5). Victoria Permanent Building Society.
        (6). Royal Arcade   „
        (7). Northern Counties   „
        (8). Grainger   „
    [476] The scarcity of building societies in Scotland is very noticeable. Cf.
H. Fawcett, "Manual of Political Economy." 6th edit., II, x, p. 276.

" way my experience teaches me that building societies have " been of great service indeed to the working classes." If this testimony is confirmed by the general experience of building societies, it would appear that the hindrance to free migration to which Dr. Fraser alluded is not one of any appreciable extent.

Another instance of a trade localised in considerable strength in different centres is that with which the Boilermakers' and Iron Shipbuilders' Society is concerned. The secretary of the society writes in these terms : " Our members go all over the United " Kingdom to work. We get to know where they are wanted " through our branches, and then pay their fares to the situa- " tions."[47] During the recent strike on the Tyne and the Wear, an actual instance of this kind of migration appeared in one of the local papers. A paragraph in an issue of the "Newcastle Daily " Chronicle" stated that the Sunderland representative of the society had received an application from a shipbuilding firm at Southampton for six squads of men and a "beam-smith" (19 men in all) to go there on favourable wages, and that the number of workmen required had been despatched. This firm, it was added, had obtained altogether about twelve squads of men from the Tyne, Wear, and Tees district during the strike.

Migration of this character is of course more common during a strike or any other suspension of industry than in times when trade is brisk or regular. But, taking a general view of the trade-societies of the country, it appears that "travelling" in search of work is not now so usual as it once was. The rapidity and comparative cheapness of locomotion have had, it seems, a two-fold effect. They have facilitated migration from one centre to another; but they have diminished the force of the motives which prompt to that migration, for they have, so to say, given a cosmo-politan and international character to periods of trade depression— so much so, indeed, that at such times emigration in search of work may in some cases be as futile as migration.[48] Mr. Howell, in an article in the "Contemporary Review," says[49] that tramping in search of work has become less "customary" and also less " respectable" than it was; and that of the two classes of " donation"—as "allowance" for "out of work" is frequently termed—the "travelling relief," which was only sufficient to meet the daily expenses of a single traveller, is being rapidly superseded

<hr/>

[47] Cf. Royal Commission on the Depression of Trade. Q. 14756, 14763. Cf. for the opposite fact, that the "best men" remain in the same place and do not migrate. Q. 11165.

[48] Cf. op. cit. Q. 3408.

[49] Cf. "Contemporary Review," September, 1883, vol. xliv. "The Work of " Trades Unions," by G. Howell.

by the "home donation," in which the family can share. It is
impossible, however, to estimate the rapidity of this change, as
the figures recording the sums expended in these two directions
are placed together under one head in the accounts given in this
article.

Another industry which is similarly situated to the shipbuilding
trade is that connected with the manufacture of iron and steel.
We have already noticed the rapid development of the Cleveland
district, and the consequent immigration of miners and ironworkers from other parts of the country. The secretary of the
Ironworkers' Union stated to me that their industry was perhaps
more migratory than any other; for, with the exception of the
higher branches of the trade, the men moved from place to place
throughout the kingdom. The reports of arbitration proceedings
contain some testimony to a similar effect. Workmen state
before Mr. Dale in 1877 that they had come from Staffordshire
into the district;[480] and the employers argue before Mr. Watson in
1884 that in the times when there was a "great demand for iron
"rails" it "was necessary" to attract men "to the north" by
extra-rates of wages.[481] One employer, indeed, says,[482] before
Sir Joseph Pease in 1882, that "some years ago" he had taken
the "trouble of looking into" the "books" of his firm "to see
"how many puddlers were employed during the year," and he
found that "there passed through" their "books in the course of
"the twelve months just about three times the number that" they
"employed each day. That showed," he added, "the habit of
"migration—working only a few days here and there, and then
"going away."

(2). We may now pass on to another class of industries—those
which are not concentrated in any exceptional strength at one
place rather than another, but are dispersed throughout the length
and breadth of the land. And first the trades which may be
included under the general name of the building trades claim
attention. There is naturally some temporary migration connected with these trades which it is scarcely necessary to notice.
If a contract of great magnitude is undertaken by a building firm,
the men employed may, in some instances, migrate to the district
where the work is carried on. An instance of a movement somewhat
analogous to this in general character has been supplied to me by
two officials connected with the Trades Councils in Edinburgh and
Glasgow. They both agree in stating that the masons in their
districts in many cases cross the Atlantic for the summer season
to obtain employment in the United States of America, and return

480 Cf. I, p. 14.   481 Cf. VI, p. 7.   482 Cf. IV, p. 18.

home for the winter; and the Glasgow writer adds that bricklayers often follow the same custom. But we are not concerned so much with this kind of migration as with that of a more permanent character. The secretary of the Amalgamated Society of Carpenters and Joiners states that joiners are "made" in small towns, and "consequently migrate" to the large towns when young and there "settle down." He adds, however, that "few trades, if any, " swell the ranks of emigration so much " as his; and in a discussion at the Industrial Remuneration Conference he is reported to have said[183] that "it was now an uncommon thing for a man to be " found in a shop for more than eighteen months or two years " together."

Somewhat similar to the building trades in its distribution in different localities is the printing trade. Here however there is apparently not so much migration. The trade societies (the most important of which seem to be the London Society of Compositors in the metropolis, and the Typographical Association in the provinces) in this industry, as in most others, provide "travelling " relief;" and the secretary of the Typographical Association says— speaking generally of all trades—that full advantage is taken of this provision. But the secretary of the London Society of Compositors states that "since the abolition of the vicious system " of tramping some few years ago," the members of his society have been "discouraged from leaving London *in search*[184] of " employment;" and that, though permission has been given to spend 300*l*. a year in emigration to the colonies, the largest sum expended in this direction was 271*l*. in 1879.

In trades which are of a more domestic nature, the secretary of the Boot and Shoe Riveters and Finishers says that men " move " from town to town in search " of employment; that " three- " fourths of these journeys are made upon foot irrespective of " distance," and that "young men frequently leave their homes in " order to obtain a wide knowledge of the trade, picking up " " experience in every town and shop in which they work ;" and that they thus become " unsteady " in habits and continue so until marriage.[185] In the tailoring trade, on the other hand, it appears that formerly about 75 per cent. of the men went "on the road " after their term of apprenticeship was over, to obtain a thorough knowledge of the trade, but that this habit has become much less prevalent of recent years.

In conclusion, we must not forget to notice some incidental influences affecting migration. An engineer, for instance, will

---

[183] *Cf.* Industrial Remuneration Conference Report, p. 333.
[184] The *italics* are my own.
[185] *Cf. op. cit.*, p. 210.

often be sent out on a ship by the firm which has constructed the
engines; and it has been said that it will be generally found that
the engineer of a steamer is a Newcastle man. Or, again, the
well-known firm of Sir William Armstrong and Company is largely
engaged in the manufacture and erection of hydraulic cranes, and
the firm will send a man or men of their own to take charge of
these cranes in different parts of the country.

(iii) (a). The second kind of migration which calls for inquiry
is the movement from one trade to another. From an economic
point of view this may take place in two ways. A man who is
already employed in one trade may himself move into another, or
he may place his children at a different trade from that which he
himself entered.

Of these two kinds, the first seems to be so limited in extent
that it may almost be disregarded. There are several difficulties—
some natural, some, perhaps, artificial—in the way of such migration. Unskilled labour, indeed, may move from one employment
to another of the class on which the common labourer is engaged;
but there seems to be little migration from the ranks of unskilled
to those of skilled labour. The migration seems rather to be in
the contrary direction; and those who cannot find employment in
their own trades, are only too liable to fall into the unfortunate
class of unskilled labourers.[486] Thus the secretary of the Northumberland Miners' Mutual Confident Association writes of the miners
in his county—who may perhaps be termed a skilled class of
unskilled labour—that they "seldom move into other trades," and
that, if they do take this step, they turn to shipbuilding or to
factory labour, and enter the yards or the factories "as *labourers*[487]
"with the intention of working their way into higher grades."
But he adds that the number of hewers who move from the mines
into these trades does not amount to more than "from 3 to 5 per
"cent.;" and the secretary of the Durham Cokemen's Association
says that when once the men in his trade "settle down" and learn
to practise their trade with efficiency, they "scarcely ever" seek
any other employment. But, should they leave through "slackness
"of trade" or "other causes," they generally endeavour to obtain
"employment at the blast-furnaces and ship-yards on the Tyne
"and Wear," returning however for the most part back to the
coke yards because the work there is as well paid and is more
regular in its character. We hear, again, of agricultural labourers
coming from the country into the steel trade which has been
opened to comparatively unskilled labour by the Bessemer and

---

[486] *Cf.* First Report of the Royal Commission on the Depression of Trade,
App. A, p. 95, *Ans.* 2. *Cf.* Also Second Report, part 1, App. B, p. 403, *Ans.* 4.
[487] The *italics* are my own.

Gilchrist-Thomas and other processes of manufacture. And, if we require an instance of the "degradation"—using the word in its etymological meaning—of skilled labour to the ranks and the occupation of unskilled, we may find it in the statement of the secretary of the Amalgamated Association of Operative Cotton Spinners, when he says that men "rarely, if ever," migrate from the cotton spinning trade into another, except when they are advanced in years, and then they turn to "hawking" or any employment that they can obtain.

In the case of skilled labour, the barrier between trade and trade is, as we have said, partly natural and partly also perhaps artificial. In most industrial occupations special skill of a high degree is needed; and this takes time to acquire. The division of labour, indeed, has gone so far that one branch of a trade is now as sternly separated from another as in former times trade was distinguished from trade. In the leather industry, for example, it appears that a currier would not be employed in dressing seal-skins unless he had had special training and experience in the *particular* method of dressing applied to these skins. In the manufacture of the pianoforte it is stated[468] in the report of the Industrial Remuneration Conference that some men are entirely engaged in the work of "cleaning off and preparing for the "polisher." The former secretary of the Amalgamated Society of Engineers, who has been recently appointed to conduct[469] the arrangements and action of the Labour Department of the newly-created "Bureau of Labour Statistics," says that even when trades are "closely analogous—such as cabinet-making, "pattern-making, house-joinering, and machine-joinering—there "is very little moving from one to another." The secretary of the London Society of Compositors "knows of no" instance "where compositors have become skilled artisans in any other "trade," though they may sometimes start in business for themselves, relying upon the knowledge and experience of others, and often of their own wives. The secretary of the Cotton Spinners states that the members of his society "never"—so far as his "experience" goes—turn from one branch of the trade to another. The Secretary of the Amalgamated Society of Carpenters and Joiners says that the members of his society "do not leave" their "trade for any other," nor yet for any other "grade," unless they are compelled to adapt themselves to "natural changes brought "about by scientific improvements." If they do leave the trade, he adds, they generally "join the army" of "public officials" and "distributors." On the other hand, it seems that in the boot and

shoe trade men "frequently" come into the trade from other
industries in consequence of the "facilities" afforded for learning
the trade by its domestic character and its extreme subdivision.
But, the secretary of the union adds, "very few" leave the trade
to enter another.

(b). The system of apprenticeship, which is still acknowledged,
in theory at least, and—if we may draw any conclusions from the
answers furnished by the secretaries of local "lodges" to the
Royal Commission on the Depression of Trade[490]—to a considerable
extent also in practice,[491] accentuates this line of separation between
trade and trade, and one branch and another of the same trade.
The period of seven years, which seems also to be frequently
observed—despite of many exceptions—renders it unlikely that a
man will be willing, even if he is able, to sacrifice the advantage
he has gained from seven years' special training,[492] and to spend
another seven years of his life upon a fresh training.

And here too the practice of subdivision has been carried to a
very great length. At one engineering factory, at least, in the city
of Newcastle-upon-Tyne, it appears to be still the practice to make
the apprentice a thorough "all-round" workman, by giving him a
complete knowledge of the different branches of the trade; and the
late secretary of the Society of Amalgamated Engineers writes
that there are in his trade "several branches nearly allied" to one
another, and that "many good all-round men work with equal
"readiness and skill at two or more" of these branches. But he
states that these are "exceptional," and "do not average 5 per cent.,"
and it seems to be a practice frequently followed to make a boy
acquainted with the working of only one or two lathes or machines;
and similar customs appear to prevail in other industries. A
member of the Trades Council at Hull says that movement from
trade to trade and from branch to branch is "exceptional;" but
that the latter does take place in cases where men have served
during their years of apprenticeship for some time, it may be,
to fitting, and for some time to turning, or for some time again
to fitting and some time to pattern-making. The secretary of
the Typographical Association writes that "at one time in a
"provincial town" a printer used to learn the "whole trade,"
—"case and press"—but that now the latter kind of work is
"nearly obsolete," and that there is a "sharp" division drawn
between "compositors" and "machine-men," and in a few excep-

[490] Cf. Second Report, part ii, App. D.
[491] It is to be noticed that in many cases there appear to be no formal
indentures.
[492] Cf. on the "manufacture" of a skilled workman, op. cit., Q. 3362.
Cf. also Q. 6529, 6531.

tional cases alone the "machine-man" combines both branches of the trade. It is hardly necessary to point out here that this sub-division of trades—if carried to a great length—has some tendency to limit the field of employment in the case of industrial depression; and it may well be that something of the nature of technical education may help in a measure to counteract this.[493] It probably also exercises influence, in a manner worthy of notice, on migration from town to town.

And indeed, speaking in general terms, migration from trade to trade, and migration from town to town, act and react upon one another. For, if a town has few industries, there is at once little opportunity of migration from one trade to another without leaving the town altogether, and migration into the town is limited for the most part to those who belong to the industries located there. In many small towns, for instance, the building trades are the only industries of any importance. The secretary of the London Society of Compositors, states that he was himself "apprenticed to a "printer, and learnt the three branches of 'compositor,' 'press-"'man,' and 'machine-manager.' " But when he came to London he found that those three branches were "three distinct trades," and he had to "elect" which of the three he would follow. "In "no case," he adds, "do London workmen follow more than one of "these branches," and to one alone is a boy apprenticed during the seven years he is "serving his time." A member of the Edinburgh Trades Council writes to a similar effect. He says that in his own trade (that of a type-founder) a man begins as a "learner," and "continually" changes to the "other stages of the trade," and can therefore work at any grade. But in "other trades—such "as blacksmiths, joiners, masons, and engineers"—the practice varies according as the time of apprenticeship is served in town or in country. These trades, it seems, are largely "recruited" from the country districts; and, when the apprenticeship is served with a "small country-employer," the workmen are taught all the branches of the trade, and are consequently able to turn from one branch to another, if trade should be dull in one branch and better in another. But, when the apprenticeship is served in the town, only one department of the trade is usually learnt, and the men therefore become "specialists," and cannot "shift" from branch to branch. Thus the traditions of different districts vary. In the South of England, we have been told, a man is trained in one class of trade, to be a tin-smith, and nothing beyond; if he migrates to the North he will perhaps practise gas-fitting and plumbing as well; and if he then returns southwards he will there find that plumbers

[493] *Cf.* Report of the Royal Commission on the Depression of Trade, Q. 8049..

" do glazing-work ;" and, if he once more turns his footsteps north-
wards, he will discover that here glaziers engage in painting.

(c). Within the ranks of a trade itself it seems that in many
cases there are not a few opportunities of rising from a lower to
a higher grade.   The secretary of the Northumberland Miners'
Union says, that " from 90 to 95 per cent. of the Northumbrian
" miners enter the mine " at " 12 to 13 " years of age, and begin as
" doorkeepers, flatters (?) or switchers," receiving from 1s. to 1s. 3d.
for a working day of ten hours.   They next pass on to " driving,"
then to " putting " or " hauling " at " 15 to 16 years of age," and
at this work they " continue " until they reach the age of 19 or 20,
and receive in wages from 2s. 11d. to 3s. 8d. for a day's work of
ten hours.   From putting, &c., they pass on to " hewing," at about
the age of 20, and this is the " highest grade " to which " 90 to 95
" per cent. of them " can ever " hope " to attain.   For " in a mine
" employing from 100 to 250 hewers there are never more than two
" ' overmen,' and there is also one ' deputy ' for every 18 or 20
" ' hewers.' "   These " deputies," however, are " invariably "
selected from the " hewers," and the " overmen " in their turn
from the " deputies."   In the Durham coke trade, the secretary of
the men's association states that the sons of cokemen, who enter
their father's trade, are employed in " light work " " above bank,"
and are then in some cases transferred at 17 or 18 years of age to
" small (?) running " or " overloading," and from that to " coke-
" drawing."   In cotton spinning, " overlookers, &c., are almost
" invariably taken from the ranks."   In the printing trade, the
secretary of the Typographical Association says that the positions
of " overseer " and " sub-overseer " are " usually filled " by " men
" who have risen " from the status of " journeymen ;" and the
secretary of the London Society of Compositors writes that " com-
" positors, as a rule, become ' readers,' ' storekeepers,' ' overseers,'
" ' managers,' ' printer's clerks,' ' travellers,' &c. ;" and he also
mentions the interesting fact that " not a few " " literary men "
have " originally " been compositors.   In the manufactured iron
trade men move from grade to grade, but the process occupies
some years, and is retarded and limited by the fact that there are
comparatively few members of the higher grades.[494]   In the engineering industries in some departments—and " especially " that of
" machine-working "—" men frequently rise from the lower to the
" higher grades."   " A skilful, intelligent man," writes the late
secretary of the Amalgamated Society of Engineers, " with natural
" aptitude, is sure to rise from a low grade to a higher, provided
" of course he is steady and reliable."   In the boilermaking and

[494] *Cf.* IV, p. 21.

iron-shipbuilding "industry there are five branches:—(1) "angle "iron smiths," (2) "platers," (3) "riveters," (4) "caulkers," (5) "holders-up." Men "move upwards" from the lowest grade, which is the last-mentioned one of the five, "as circumstances "permit." A member of the higher branch does not often accept work in a lower branch, unless indeed trade is "slack" in his own branch and "brisk" in the other; and a rule of the society prohibits him from acting in this way "if there is any man of the "lower branch out of work in the district."

(*d*). This rule, which is very similar to a regulation amongst the engineers, requiring "every member to work as nearly as "possible at his own branch," naturally conducts us to the consideration of another question; and that is the extent to which trades unions restrict the migration of labour by their conditions with regard to apprenticeship. Very many, if not most, of these associations have rules regulating the admission of new members, and these rules appear in many cases to contain a reference to apprenticeship.

But it seems doubtful whether in practice the actual production of an indenture of apprenticeship is required. The chief requisite appears to be evidence of ability to earn the wages current in the district, and this evidence is obtained, it seems, by the testimony of members of the society who have worked side by side with the candidate for admission. Nor is the production of an indenture of apprenticeship invariably regarded as adequate evidence of this ability; for there is an impression—perhaps not unreasonable—whether the fault be ascribed to the workman himself or to his teacher, or to the system of instruction—that the fact that a man has "served his time" is no proof that he has learnt his trade. And, in the case of a stranger, it is apparently often the practice that he should not be admitted to the society until he has spent a certain time in the district, and has given his fellow-workmen opportunity of discovering his working qualities—a practice, it may be noticed, which has the collateral advantage of enabling the new-comer to earn sufficient wages to pay his entrance-fee.

And on this last point it may be remarked that the combination of the "friendly-society" with the "trade-society" in a "trade "union"—strenuously as it has been assailed, and stoutly as it has been defended, on other grounds—seems to be likely to operate in a manner which appears to have escaped detection. For, as the friendly-society payments must, if calculated on a sound actuarial basis, vary according to the age of the new member, they may, in some cases, be prohibitive to a candidate for admission. And, if the unionist feeling is so strong in the district as to present moral, if not actual, obstacles to his entrance into the trade as a non-

unionist workman, it may prevent his adoption of a trade for
which he is otherwise qualified. Thus, to take a single instance,
in the Typographical Association it seems[495] that the amount of
entrance fee payable on joining the association varies from 5*s.* for
those under 40 years of age, to 7*s.* 6*d.* for those over 40 and under
45, and 10*s.* for those over 45 and under 50, and for those over 50
it amounts to 1*l.*

How far trades unionists have the power or desire to exclude
non-unionists from an industry or district it is scarcely possible to
determine. There has in all probability been no little exaggeration upon the point, and, if we may believe Mr. Howell's estimate
of the strength of unionism, it does not seem to be likely, or
indeed possible, that a body of one-third can *absolutely* control the
action of a body of men of twice that number. Unionists may
however be concentrated in great strength in particular localities,
and may there use moral, perhaps actual, compulsion to exclude
non-unionists. But on the whole there seems to be more elasticity
in the principles and practice of unionism than is popularly
supposed.

Mr. Howell in his valuable work on trades unions, published in
1878, has gone through[496] the rules and action of the chief trade
societies. He mentions stringent rules[497] as existing amongst the
boilermakers and iron-shipbuilders, strictly limiting the number
of apprentices, and the age of admission to the trade. If we may
repose any confidence in local *hearsay*, these rules seem to be
enforced, in spirit at least, with some rigour in the Newcastle
district. They appear at any rate to exclude the labourers in the
yards from any but the most uncertain hope of rising to higher
occupations. But Mr. Howell states[498] that the exclusive rules of
the boiler-makers are "practically dormant."

He also alludes to very strict limitations on the number of
apprentices among the hatters,[499] and in the printing trade; and
in the case of the latter industry the secretaries of the London
Society of Compositors and the Typographical Association bear
similar testimony. But Mr. Howell himself says[500] that, despite of
organised attempts to secure the observance of these rules, they
cannot be rigorously enforced in practice; and the missionary

[495] *Cf.* Rules of the Typographical Association (as amended by the vote of
the members, March, 1886), XII, 1.
[496] *Cf.* "Conflicts of Capital and Labour," by G. Howell, ch. V, sec. 24—74.
[497] *Cf. op. cit.,* sec. 29.
[498] *Cf. op. cit.,* sec. 29. *Cf.* Report of the Royal Commission on the Depression of Trade, Q. 11923—29.
[499] *Cf. op. cit.,* sec. 46 and 39—43.
[500] *Cf. op. cit.,* sec. 40.

efforts recorded[501] in the Half-Yearly Report of the Typographical Association for the latter part of the year 1885, and strennously urged[502] in a letter inserted in the "Typographical Circular," the organ of the Association, in May, 1886, seem to show that the Association has not sufficient strength to make its rules the *universal* invariable practice of the *whole* of the trade. In many other cases it appears that rules, nominally in existence, are practically obsolete; and in some instances—such as the iron-workers, the carpenters, and the factory operatives—even nominal rules do not seem to be found.

The whole policy of apprenticeship, indeed, is one about which there is no little difficulty in arriving at a correct decision. On the one hand it seems that the traditional period of seven years can hardly be required for learning merely a branch of a trade. On the other hand trades unions have as much right to demand evidence of efficiency as a condition of membership, as inns of court and colleges of physicians and surgeons have to enforce the test of examination. They may even be conferring as much service upon the public in securing efficient workmen, as the "professional "trades unions"—as they are sometimes called—presumably confer by prohibiting, as far as they can, unqualified practitioners. But the "professional trades unions" endeavour to secure quality rather than to restrict quantity, while the industrial trades unions, in theory at least, aim in some cases at the restriction of quantity; and the historical antecedents of the policy of apprenticeship (as practised by the mediæval guilds in their degenerate days) point to a similar object as only too likely to be adopted. On the other hand, again, it is difficult, as we have seen, even in cases where these rules exist, to discover how far they are, or can be, rigidly enforced in practice, and how far they are the result of an avowed or tacit agreement between masters and men. For almost every trade has its own unwritten law, and with the details of this it is difficult for the lay mind to obtain acquaintance.

(e). So far, however, as the rules limiting the number of apprentices are enforced from the point of view of enlightened, or unenlightened, selfishness, they raise another question of great interest but of equal obscurity—the question how far do or do not children follow the occupations of their parents. There can be little doubt that here, as on other points connected with the migration of labour, economic considerations exercise an appreciable effect. But it is equally certain that here, as elsewhere, there is no small amount of "friction" to be taken into account.

[501] *Cf.* Seventy-third Half-yearly Report of the Typographical Association, pp. 3 and 4.

[502] *Cf.* Typographical Circular, No. 404, p. 4.

The information which can be gathered upon the question is of the vaguest description. On the one side there is the familiar impression felt and expressed by many, if not most, men, that they themselves would have done better had they pursued any other occupation than that which they have actually followed. They therefore desire to give their children a better chance than they have themselves enjoyed, by placing them at another trade. They are acquainted—only too well acquainted, as they think—with the disadvantages and drawbacks of their own trade. And the promise held out by another trade has an attractive glamour lent to it by the distance from which it is surveyed—a glamour which perhaps might be dispelled by closer familiarity. Thus, to take a single instance, we find constant references before arbitrators to the unwillingness evinced—and in this case at least not unreasonably evinced—by puddlers to place their sons in their own trade. Nor is an unskilled labourer likely, if he can help it, to allow his children to remain in the ranks of the common labourers.

On the other hand a man has in all probability more opportunities of securing a favourable start for his children in the race of life in his own occupation than in any other. The secretary of the Amalgamated Association of Operative Cotton Spinners "would say" that in his trade "about three-fourths" of the children follow the same occupation as their fathers; the secretary of the Boilermakers and Iron-shipbuilders states that "most" of their members' sons are brought up to their father's trade. The secretary of the National Union of Operative Boot and Shoe Riveters and Finishers affirms that the children in his trade follow in a great measure the same trade as their fathers, and adds that, in view of the fact that the trade is "more or less localised," in some cases there is no alternative industry to enter; and the late secretary of the Amalgamated Society of Engineers also writes that children to "a large extent" follow their fathers' trades; for, he adds, "it is generally easiest for a father to get his son into his own "trade," and "in very many special cases no other trade or even "branch of trade is open" to him. Nor must we forget that some allowance must be made for the special aptitude for special occupations which seems, in some cases at least, to be almost a matter of inheritance,[503] and to be beyond the power of alien blood to acquire with adequate perfection.

In the case of the printing trade both the opposing motives we have mentioned appear to be present, and to conflict with one another. On the one side it seems that the stringent rules about apprenticeship have been at times relaxed in favour of the eldest

---

[503] *Cf.* Report of the Royal Commission on the Depression of Trade, *Q.* 3366.

son of a compositor, who might exercise the "privilege" of serving "without indentures."[501] But on the other side the secretary of the London Society of Compositors writes that, though "the eldest "son" of a compositor is "sometimes a compositor" himself, yet as "a general rule" "compositors' sons do not follow their fathers' "occupation." There is, he adds, such a strong sense of the mischief done to the interests of the men by the plethora of "boy-labour" in the trade, that "many compositors would hesitate before intro- "ducing another lad, even though he be his own son." The secretary of the Typographical Association states that there is not any noteworthy evidence upon either the one side of the question or the other. The secretary, in the last place, of the Amalgamated Society of Carpenters and Joiners says that the question "depends "very largely" upon the condition of the trade. If it is pros- perous, then the children enter it ; if it is depressed, their fathers will place them at any occupation in preference to their own.

(iv). This collection of opinion and facts upon the question of the migration of labour—though falling far short of completeness —is, we may hope, tolerably comprehensive in the variety and number of industries to which it relates, and may perhaps be regarded as being, in some measure at least, typical of the leading characteristics of the industrial world of modern England. Difficult as it is to arrive at detailed accuracy, and conflicting as some of the evidence seems to be, two general conclusions may nevertheless be drawn. In the first place it would be hardly possible, without the assistance of a preliminary hypothesis, to evolve by any purely inductive process—if such a process indeed be in any case really possible—a satisfactory theory of value out of such a collection of materials. The second conclusion is this, that different industries have different characteristics.

And thus we are led back to the proposition from which we originally started, that methods of industrial reform must be mani- fold and not single, must exhibit diversity and not uniformity of detail, must admit, in short, of application to the varying circum- stances of different industries. This is the lesson which has, it would seem, to be learnt by enthusiastic optimists and despondent pessimists alike. It is a hard lesson indeed ; but it is also a lesson which is full of hope and abounding in promise, if once it is thoroughly learnt.

[501] Cf. "Conflicts of Capital and Labour," chap. v, sec. 39.

HARRISON AND SONS, PRINTERS IN ORDINARY TO HER MAJESTY, ST. MARTIN'S LANE.